LEARNING TO LOVE YOURSELF

*The Steps To Self-Acceptance,
The Path To Creative Fulfillment*

Gay Hendricks, Ph.D.

D0188756

TABLE OF CONTENTS

Introducing The New Edition

I am thrilled and delighted to offer to you the new edition of *Learning To Love Yourself*. Revisiting and rewriting the book has been a pleasure from beginning to end. With its new elements, the book comes alive in a whole new way.

Looking back over more than three decades to the moment of its conception, I can now see how writing this book changed my life in every way. I first wrote it as an act of love, to share an experience that still even now feels as if it's still transforming me in my very cells. It was my hope that telling about the experience could inspire the same profound life-changes in others. The many thousands of letters, emails and spoken appreciations I've received since then let me know that my hope came true.

The experience described in the book revealed the living mystery of love to me, allowing me to feel its sweet power for the first time. Because I suddenly knew what real love felt like, I was able to break free of my pattern of painful relationships with women. Ultimately it helped me find my way to Kathlyn, the love of my life and my wife for the past quarter-century.

Of all my books, this is the one people ask the most detailed technical questions about. Did I write it on a typewriter? How long did the writing take? To answer these sorts of questions once and for all, I recall that the book was written on an improvised desk made from a wooden door supported by a stack of concrete blocks at either end. I was staying in David Josephson's house in Palo Alto that summer, so I could be close to Kathlyn, who had her movement studio in the living room of the house. David's spare bedroom had nothing in it but a bed and a chair, so I had to improvise. I found a wooden door in the garage, borrowed a few concrete blocks from a neighbor, and poof: instant desk!

It was the first summer of my relationship with Kathlyn. I worked on the book every morning, then spent as much time as possible with her in the afternoons and evenings. Those were the pre-computer days, of course, and I never liked writing my books on a typewriter. Every word of *Learning To Love Yourself* was written on yellow legal pads with my beloved 19-cent Bic pens, the clear plastic kind they don't make anymore.

Although I had published several books before *Learning To Love Yourself*, this was the first one I felt passionate about writing. I poured my heart and soul into every sentence of the book. Instead of writing with thoughtful distance and careful analysis, the style so revered in my Stanford Ph.D. training, I hurled myself into the maelstrom of my own confusion, anxieties and joys. I described as intimately as I could the ecstasies and agonies that gripped me. My only criterion was truth. At the end of a sentence I would pause and ask myself, "Is that absolutely, unarguably true?" If I got a clear 'yes,' I went on to write the next sentence. When I finished the book I felt for the first time in my career that I had fulfilled my creative potential.

The book changed my life in many other ways, some of which took me by surprise and turned my life in unfamiliar directions. When first published in 1982, it was subjected to a scathing review in a then-popular magazine, *Psychology Today*. Through the sweetest of ironies, this awful review produced an unimaginably wonderful outcome for me. To understand what happened, I should tell you that self-help books were rare in those early days, and to my knowledge there had never been one in which the author revealed his or her own feelings to the extent that I did in this book. It was this deeply personal aspect that so outraged the reviewer in *Psychology Today*, one R. D. Rosen.

I remember it was a Sunday afternoon when a friend, Ed Graham, called me to ask if I had seen the latest *Psychology Today*. I told him I hadn't. "Do yourself a favor," Ed said. "Don't read it." He went on to tell me that the review of my new book wasn't exactly flattering and that I was probably better off not burdening myself with the details. *Psychology Today* wasn't a magazine I read regularly, but based on my friend's tantalizing warning I rushed down to the nearest newsstand to get it. I didn't even wait to purchase the magazine, so eager was I to devour the forbidden fruit. Standing by the magazine rack, I flipped through the pages until I came to the review, which I read at first eagerly, then with morbid fascination. It was then that I first learned of the pain and suffering I had inflicted upon R. D. Rosen.

Rosen not only hated the book (and the emerging self-help genre in general), he intimated that I had lost my mind and sacrificed my academic reputation by sharing my own feelings of anger, anxiety and longing. In one particularly vivid passage, he even shared some feelings of his own, saying that parts of my book were so personal that they made him sick to his stomach! (I heard later that he was a part-time restaurant critic. For him to say it made him sick to his stomach was harsh criticism indeed.)

By the time I finished reading the review I wasn't feeling in the best of moods, either. I slunk back to my house feeling that a hit-and-run driver had run over my career. I was a tenured professor at a major university. I had written a textbook in my field of counseling/clinical psychology, as well as many articles in scientific journals. After the breakthrough experience I described in *Learning To Love Yourself*, I felt that I had the key to bringing a much-needed wave of authenticity and emotional expression to the academic world. I loved the university world. My role in it, teaching graduate students in a counseling psychology program, was something I loved to do. The harsh reality, however, was that the *Psychology Today* review would likely be read by more people than had read all my scientific articles and textbook combined. Was I going to become a laughing-stock?

Now for the sweet irony: After the *Psychology Today* review came out, the book took off like a rocket in the marketplace. Sales doubled the next month, then tripled. I discovered the truth of the Bob Dylan quote, "There's no such thing as bad publicity." Apparently the reading public liked the very things that had turned the reviewer's stomach. I began to get tear-drenched letters of appreciation from people who thanked me for baring my soul, saying that the book had healed them by giving them permission to bare theirs. I received letters from other professors saying that I'd restored their faith in the academic world and given them a reason to go on teaching. The book became a steady bestseller, going through more than twenty printings over the next two decades.

R.D. Rosen, if you are still out there somewhere, I owe you a deep bow of gratitude and a long-overdue gift bottle of Pepto-Bismol. I also have a heartfelt request: Please review more of my books!

The best was yet to come: After the book became a bestseller I was inundated with requests to do talks and seminars. I fell into a pattern of teaching all week at the university, then flying off somewhere to do a talk or seminar on the weekend. One winter a few years after the book came out, I went to Hawaii to teach a seminar. I got off the plane and stood on the tarmac luxuriating in the 80-degree warmth of Kauai. Moments later my hosts handed me a message from my secretary back in Colorado. Someone named Oprah Winfrey had called. I should mention that there was a long stretch of my life when I didn't own a TV set, so I was far out of touch with goings-on in the popular media. According to my secretary, who devoured *People Magazine* each week, Oprah was a budding talk show host in Chicago who was starting to get national attention with her show. They wanted to do a show on the theme of *Learning To Love Yourself*. Was there any possibility I could turn around and come back to Chicago to appear on her show?

It was the month of February. I had just fled frigid Colorado to enjoy a week of Kauai sunshine. I stared at the message, pondering the idea of taking a ten-hour plane ride back to the Midwest.

My pondering lasted about half a second. I called my secretary and told her to decline. Later that day, visiting Shakti Gawain's house on Kauai, I discovered that Shakti had appeared on the show and sold hundreds of thousands of books as a result. Suddenly winter seemed a lot more appealing to me, but I resisted the temptation and stuck with my decision to stay in Hawaii. Apparently declining the offer did not terminally offend the show's producers, because later they were kind enough to have both Kathlyn and me for several appearances. We were blessed with great book sales, but the appearances on Oprah and other shows led to something far more rewarding: the founding of our own institute. As a result of the increased visibility, we got requests from hundreds of therapists, M.D.s and other professionals who wanted to study with us. Soon, we were offering training seminars in North America, Asia and Europe to accommodate those requests. The Hendricks

Institute has grown over the past twenty years to become a thriving training center that graduates several hundred professionals a year as well as offering seminars to growth-oriented laypersons, about 20,000 of whom have honored us with their participation.

Now, a new version makes it way out into the world. It has been updated, rearranged and polished according to new things I've learned over the years. Readers of the original book will notice a major difference right away. When I first wrote *Learning To Love Yourself*, I began the book by describing the moment of learning to love myself that the whole book hinged upon. When Lynne, my editor at Prentice-Hall, sent back the edited manuscript, she insisted that I put this description at the back of the book. She felt strongly that many readers would be put off by such a personal account of a life-changing moment. She believed that readers wanted the concepts and techniques, not the personal experiences they were based on. She and I went 'round and 'round about this issue, but in the end she prevailed. I was young and opinionated but she was more experienced (as well as more opinionated!) She also had another thing going for her: the checkbook. She wouldn't officially accept the manuscript and pay me the rest of the advance money unless I agreed to her sequencing of the book. After weighing the options (hunger vs. letting her be right) I decided to do it her way. Now, in a life-stage in which I'm much less hungry and much more opinionated, I am restoring the chapters to their original sequence.

Regardless of the sequence, the heart and soul of the book was, is and always shall be a simple, loving description of a moment that changed everything for me. My high intention for this book is that it will do the same for you.

With love,
Gay Hendricks
Ojai, California,
May, 2006

CHAPTER ONE
How I Learned To Love Myself

One day in the autumn of my twenty-ninth year, I had a life-changing experience, my first clear moment of loving myself. Since this moment is the source of everything in this book, I'd like to describe it in detail.

Here is what happened:

Prior to that day, I had spent the better part of two weeks alone in a cabin in Green Mountain Falls, near Colorado Springs. My days had been spent in meditation, long hikes and self-reflection. It was the first time I had slowed down to take a look at my life in many years. I had just earned my Ph.D. from Stanford and was about to start my professional career as a professor at University of Colorado. I had moved from California, my home for the previous few years, to a place where I knew almost nobody. I had left behind friends, family, a close woman friend, and a life that had meant much to me. Somehow I had thought that coming to a new place would allow me to start clean and afresh. Those two weeks alone had shown me, though, something I was having a hard time facing: until I came to terms with myself internally, I could travel to the ends of the earth and not feel at peace. During the two weeks alone I had gone through many cycles of pain, loneliness, and fear, with an occasional flash of joy to illuminate the days and nights.

I was at a crisis point in my work. For many years I had been searching for the answer to one question: How can we bring about change in ourselves? I wanted to know the most fundamental processes by which we could transform ourselves, our relationships and the world around us. This question had propelled me into counseling psychology and all the way to a doctorate; it had sent me to hundreds of lectures, thousands of books and journals, and dozens of professors, gurus, and sages. I still did not know the answer. Actually, I knew many theories and facts, but I knew nothing that resonated in my own heart and mind. Now the question was gaining urgency, because I was about to start my new job as a professor in charge of training therapists. In a week I would stand up in front of my first graduate school class. Although I had my bottomless grab bag of facts and theories, I knew I was not going to feel satisfied spouting the accumulated wisdom of my field. I wanted to be able to teach what I knew to be true from my own experience.

THE MOMENT

I was sauntering along a mountain path when the moment came upon me. It popped into my mind that the Buddha decided to sit under a tree until he reached enlightenment. In that moment I decided I to stop and wait until I had my answers. In a flash I realized I had been looking outside myself for the answers. I had never really turned the question over to my own experience. I had asked everyone except myself. Suddenly my mind grew still and electric, like the air just before a thunderstorm. To ask myself, to trust my own experience—it seemed so outrageous an idea that I did it on the spot then and there.

I phrased a question in my mind:

What is the one thing we can do to bring about transformation?

Another question spontaneously bubbled up:

How can I deal with negative feelings so that they do not recycle?

Then another: What is the one thing I could do to make my life flow freely and easily?

A second or two later the answers to those questions shot through me, not intellectually but in the form of an electric wave of ecstatic sensation that swept up my body from my legs to my head. I reeled about under the trees, staggered by the impact of the energy. I felt as if a benign freight-train of energy was roaring through my body. How I greeted the energy made a difference in how it felt. If I relaxed my body and moved around and let the energy dance its way through me, I felt the energy as an ecstatic, good feeling. If I tensed against it or stopped letting myself move with the energy, I didn't feel as good. The energy continued to pulsate through me for the better part of an hour while I moved and danced and flexed my body in the stillness of the forest. After a while the energy subsided, and I discovered to my great delight and surprise that I now had all the answers to my questions. I felt a deep conceptual knowing of the answers along with a sense of joy and fulfillment in my body. It felt as if the energy had left behind a permanent imprint of the answers within me.

Over the next few minutes I savored the answers to my big questions. I also discovered that if I wished to know more about any of the questions, all I had to do was to relax into the energy in my body and the answers appeared spontaneously in my mind. It was a whole new way of knowing, and it felt deeply nourishing.

First, here was the answer to my question about how to deal with all the feelings of anger and sadness that recycled in me. The answer was simple: Feel the feelings in your body— don't conceptualize about them in your mind. Be with them by directing sensitive awareness toward them. Feel them as intensely as you can, and love yourself for feeling them. I was stunned by this answer. All my life I had been trying to figure out with my mind how to deal with feelings, and now I realized that the way to deal with them was not a mental thing at all! I had been trapped by my proud intellect into thinking there was some way to deal with feelings through a mental manipulation. The answer indicated that feelings had only to be felt; the solution was beyond the mind. It was so foreign to my ordinary way of thinking that I went ahead and did it on the spot.

Instead of trying to talk myself out of my feelings as I had always done, I simply stood there and allowed all my feelings to wash over me. I surrendered to loneliness, fear, and longing. I invited up all the anger that I had always suppressed behind my nice-guy facade. Waves of anguish and sadness swelled up from my chest and suffused me. I simply opened myself to whatever was there. For perhaps a half-hour I stood under the trees and danced with the waves of feeling as they came up. My body was a torrent of emotion and conflict until suddenly everything subsided and I felt a warm, peaceful glow throughout my body and mind. Then the glow turned into a rush of exhilaration as I realized what I had learned.

Along with the answer to how to deal with feelings had come the answer to my question about the one thing that brings about transformation. I saw very clearly that *resistance* keeps life painful and complicated. I had been resisting reality all my life—resisting facing it, resisting accepting it, resisting feeling it. Whenever I would have a feeling, like fear, I would immediately tense against it and try to make it go away. It seemed that my whole life was one big resistance: against my feelings, against love, against my own energy and potential. In that moment I decided to stop resisting. Suddenly everything changed. The moment I stopped resisting I could greet all of myself with love. I opened up to accept the previously unloved parts of myself. After all, what did those parts of me need if not my love? When I dropped my stance of resistance, I felt totally connected to myself. I was free and alive, suddenly moving with the river instead of against it. It was, I believe, my life's first conscious moment of peace. It was my rebirth-day.

IN PRACTICE

I want to explore resistance further because it felt at the time, and still does, to be the monumental problem we encounter in our psychological growth. Throughout our lives we have experiences such as fear, sadness, sexuality, things we want, creative urges. We learn to resist these experiences, either because we are told to resist them by parents and society, or because we do not know what to do with the experiences at the time. Take sexuality as an example. We may resist our sexual feelings because we have received overt or covert messages from other people that we should not allow ourselves to experience our sexuality. Even in the absence of such messages, though, we may decide on our own to resist sexuality because we do not know what to do with it. To open up to it would be to open Pandora's box.

When we resist our experience, certain predictable results occur. First, we lose our direct relationship with life. Since our personal experience is our direct response to life, to resist it is to begin to see life through the fog of our beliefs, opinions, and conditioned responses: through a veil of mind-stuff. We yearn for clear, direct experience; we are not satisfied with watching life through the veil. Another result of resisting our experience is that we begin to dramatize it. To continue with the example of sexuality, when we resist experiencing deeply our sexual feelings, we dramatize sexuality by fantasizing about sex, flirting, worrying about sex, and forming beliefs about sex. Freud, of course, made history by first noticing in his practice how many people who had resisted their sexuality dramatized it to the point of developing medical symptoms.

It appears, then, that one fundamental problem of life is resistance to experience. Logically the solution to this problem is to become willing to experience what we experience, and that tiny little thing is so incredibly simple yet so difficult that most people are content to live in the world of nonexperience, of drama, of shadow.

The results of that turnaround moment were manifested in my life. A few days later I did the first session of therapy I'd ever felt good about. A woman consulted me about some fears she was having, as well as about some life decisions she had to make. We dealt with the fears first. Instead of trying to talk her out of feeling scared, as I might have done the week before, I helped her open up to the fear, letting herself feel it to completion. When she came to the end of the fear, which took about fifteen minutes, a small miracle happened. The decisions she needed to make, which had seemed thorny and formidable before she let herself experience the fear, came to her mind spontaneously and effortlessly. She saw the path she had to take, the moves she had to make, the actions that were required. It was as if letting herself experience things the way they were connected her up to some inner reservoir of creativity. I was moved.

Shortly after learning to love myself that first moment, I watched another ancient pattern of my own dissolve. All my life I had craved love while simultaneously repelling it. I would get close to people, then do something to drive them away.

After that moment in the forest I saw that the old pattern was based on a deep conviction that I was unlovable. When I felt love for myself, I found that I was suddenly able to receive love from others without pushing it away at the same time. Within a week or two I met an extraordinarily loving woman with whom I developed the first truly satisfying love relationship of my life.

Now for the bad news. Learning to love ourselves means expanding to a new level of awareness, and with that awareness come new challenges. Learning to love means that we will see more that needs to be loved. When we explore a dark room with only a candle, we can see only the vague outlines of things. Give us a powerful light, though, such as the light of love, and we can see every little nook and cranny, all the dust and cobwebs, all the clutter, every imperfection. In short, we can see everything that needs to be loved. Then life becomes a process of lovingly getting that room straightened up, and you know how we hate to clean house. Love brings with it, though, a refinement of our vision. Instead of seeing the housework as a curse, we can begin to see it as a set of opportunities to expand in love. With this attitude life becomes rich and passionate.

If only there was a guarantee that learning to love meant that we could retire and never feel off-center again! Instead we can only guarantee the opposite. Learning to love yourself will bring into your awareness the very next thing that needs to be loved, and you will be stretched by it, sometimes to the limit. You will forget, as I often do, to love yourself until the very last moment, then you will remember again, only to forget again, and remember. You will get it and lose it a million times. And it really does not matter, because the essential transformation takes place at the moment you become willing to love. Being willing to love ourselves means that we are greeting life with acceptance rather than resistance. Coming at life from a stance of willingness means that you have changed the one thing that must be changed.

For me it changed everything. Life took on great joy and depth. Before that moment I felt I had been bored all my life. After that moment everything unfolded with passion. My work as a therapist and teacher became a blessing rather than a burden. It feels very good to begin each day knowing I will have the opportunity to assist people in learning to love themselves and at the same time learn to love myself more deeply.

When we experience what we are experiencing, we line ourselves up with what actually is. We stop pretending that it isn't. This is the source of much power in our lives. Masters are people who allow themselves and others to be the way they are. Accepting what is real is also the source of creativity. When we line ourselves up with what is true within ourselves, it seems to open us up to more truth. And what better thing could life be about than opening up ourselves to more power, clarity, truth, and love?

A SECOND HOLY MOMENT

That breakthrough moment under the trees gave me a sense of personal unity. After a lifetime of feeling scattered and fragmented, I felt whole. By dropping my resistance to my experience, I found myself aligned internally. I made friends with my feelings and my thoughts, and as a result I felt no further conflicts. From that moment on, I have known that whatever I experienced was all right.

This experience of inner unity set the stage for two more pivotal moments.

As I describe these experiences I find myself using words that have a spiritual connotation as well as a psychological one. It seems common for experiences in psychological growth to evolve into a spiritual quest if pursued deeply. I know that this was the case with me. I am from a secular background; my religious conditioning was so haphazardly applied as to be minimal. Yet it now seems to me perfectly natural to use terms and ideas that I would have sneered at a few years ago.

One spring morning about a year and a half after the experience in the Colorado mountains, I was walking across a college quadrangle. It was spring break, and all was quiet except for the crunch underfoot of a light snowfall from the night before. As I walked along my thoughts began to turn toward the problem of Christianity. I had just seen a book on a sale table which contained phrases that Jesus had allegedly spoken. I thought, here was a person whose message had been about love and brotherhood but which had spawned more wars than anything else in Western history. It was a message of liberation, but it had given rise to an organized church that was, in my view, monstrously oppressive. How could this all have happened? I don't know now, and I didn't know then. What happened, though, was that for some reason my mind began to see through the words and concepts about Jesus and Christianity to an experience that must have underlain it all. It occurred to me that perhaps Jesus had tapped a level of consciousness available to everyone. Certainly Jesus had seemed to say this often enough, in phrases like "Seek ye the kingdom of heaven within." Perhaps the Christ consciousness exists like a channel on a television set, ready to be dialed in by whoever chooses to take the step. I decided in that moment to take that step.

The next moment a powerful wave of energy rolled through my body, filling me with an electric feeling of exhilaration. It was a sweet feeling of heat and light. In that moment I felt boundless compassion for all humankind. My heart opened with love and gratitude to everyone. I saw all the earth and heavens as one big being, and it was the recipient of all my love. There was no separation among all beings, all nature and myself-all were equal and one. We were all together in a dance of love and celebration.

As the intensity of the feeling began to ebb, I saw an image of three paths that were open to one who taps that state of consciousness. One is the path that Jesus took: revolutionary, ending in martyrdom. Another path felt like one in which I could go about life as normal, except that the underlying context of my life could be enriched by becoming an ongoing opportunity to express love and compassion. The third path was not clear to me in the vision, although my guess is that it had something to do with the expression of that consciousness in relationships.

The effects of the experience on my life have been exciting to me. First, let me make it clear that I still have not set foot in a church, or tried to convince anybody they ought to do what I did, or done any of the tedious things that I associate with the neurotic expression of the Christ consciousness. What I have found is that most of the conflicts I formerly had with other people, and with the universe itself, seemed to clear up effortlessly. Once I saw that we were all one, that all of us were expressions of a central creative force in the universe, I found It hard to hold on to an adversary position with people around me. The experience affirmed more deeply for me something which has become central to my life. If we really want to find out the essence of religions, whether it be Buddhism or Christianity or Druidism, we must be willing to get beyond the concepts and notions about the religion and taste the underlying experience that gave rise to the religion. It surely must be the lack of a recent taste of the experience of what Christianity Is all about which sends Christians into war. Obviously, no Moslem or Hindu would set his hand against a Buddhist or Confucian if he had recently experienced the underlying unity of all religions.

THE THIRD MOMENT

The third quantum jump in my ability to love myself happened several years after the one I just described. I relate it to the first two moments because it felt connected to them by the quality of the energy I experienced in my body. All three experiences had that electric vibration that filled my body, followed by an exalted set of realizations that changed the whole context of my life.

One August night I was lying down after a half-hour's meditation. It was my custom to lie down for ten or fifteen minutes after completing my evening meditation. The period of post-meditation rest feels particularly delicious because it allows the body rest while the mind is totally silent. On this night I was enjoying the period of quiet immensely because it was a stressful time of my life. I was working hard and at the same time having a series of conflicts with my wife.

As I relaxed in the silence I began to speculate about God. I realized in that moment that practically nothing we are taught about God has any value; it is all based on someone else's experience, if indeed it is based on experience at all. I saw that what we are taught about God can, and often does, prevent us completely from inquiring into ourselves deeply enough for us to have a personal experience of God.

11

In addition, the information we get about religion is usually dispensed by organized churches with ulterior motives. Naturally, any organization that owns vast real estate holdings and plays the stock market has more than our spiritual interests at stake.

But, I thought, somewhere below all the twisted misinformation we are given about God and the spirit is perhaps an actual experience that could be tapped. After all, if I could experience myself as the created, which is by its very nature part of the creator, it made sense that I could open up to experience the driving force in the universe. First I opened myself to experiencing fully as a human, complete with anger, fear, sexuality, a body, and a mind. Then I let myself open up one more step to become willing to experience that which had created me.

Suddenly an explosion of light and vibration occurred deep inside me, and I began physically vibrating, shaking so fast and hard that it flipped me around on the bed. It felt like a powerful current passing through me. I cannot say it was a pleasant or unpleasant sensation: it was simply *present*. *I* stayed with it, breathing into it rather than resisting it, and eventually the vibrations subsided. So that's what God is, I thought. No wonder my mind had never been able to figure out what God was. God was an experience, not a concept. It was beyond the mind.

A CONCLUSION OR TWO

These experiences I've described were crucial to me because they opened up space in me which I could then choose to fill with love. It seems important to phrase it that way, because I do not feel it is important to have a particular kind of whizbang experience in order to love yourself. A moment of vivid clarity, such as those three that happened to me, can help us stand free in a space where love really makes sense out of the universe. The act of loving ourselves, though, seems outside of time and space, so that it is available to us no matter what space we are in. In other words, it is just as possible to love yourself when you are stuck as it is to love yourself when you are free. At either end of the spectrum, loving ourselves seems like the only choice we have. And regardless of how many times we go into experiences of unusual clarity, loving ourselves is something that can be applied thousands of times a week, hundreds of times a day. Perhaps it is those many little experiences of loving ourselves that make space for the big ones we experience now and then.

As I finished writing the last sentence, I realized that I had a wonderful opportunity to practice what I preach. I was feeling tired, angry at several people, and also fine and happy. I realized that loving myself had nothing to do with the way I feel. I can do it any time, regardless of circumstance. So I stood up, stretched, and loved myself to my toes. Exhilaration nearly lifted me off the ground.

CHAPTER TWO
What Are The Blocks To Loving Ourselves?

It seems obvious to me now that I am a lovable and capable person, but not too long ago I felt unlovable and ineffective. I know nothing has changed except my own mind, my own opinion of myself. The rest of the world is the same as it was, but now I see myself differently in relationship to it. It seems so natural and easy now to love myself. How did I ever make it so hard?

Perhaps we begin life in a state of being able to give and receive limitless love. Then, in the growing-up process, we make decisions about ourselves and life that cause us to fall out of love with ourselves. A decision like "I'm unlovable," made when we are two or twenty-two can affect the quality of our lives when we are thirty or sixty. I made a decision a long time ago not to trust people. I felt abandoned by my mother and father. In actual fact, he died and she went to work. Of course, I did not understand about death, bereavement, and economic necessities. To my young eyes, it looked like I was being left by people I had been relying upon. So I thought, This world is a place where people leave you just when you're counting on them. I remember feeling angry and sad about not ever seeing my father and having to share my mother with a bunch of unseen strangers every day from eight until evening. Even then she would often be tired and irritable; it was so different from the warm and happy life of a short time before.

I pulled into myself and formed a protective shell around a small part of me inside. I made a place in the corner of my grandmother's front room where I could hide from everyone, and I made a place inside me where I decided no one was going to be able to hurt me. I really did not recognize that this was a problem until I was in my late twenties, after a ruined marriage and a chain of shallow relationships. One day I woke up and saw that the little protected place where no one could hurt me was also a place where no one could touch me. I knew that if I were to be free and easy to love I had to open up that place and let it breathe fresh air, no matter what the risk.

We make decisions like "Don't trust people" to simplify the world, to make it make sense. It is safer, somehow, if we make rules. It will keep us from getting in trouble. The trouble is, of course, that in the deepest realm of life there are no rules. To make rules there instills rigidity where utmost pliability is called for.

The beauty of the human mind is that any decision that is made can be unmade. Since decisions like "Don't trust" are made only of mind-stuff, and therefore do not exist in any real sense, they can be dissolved in a flash. It is reassuring to know that any limitation you have ever installed in your mind, for whatever purpose and regardless of how long ago, can be effortlessly shed.

HOW WE COME TO FEEL UNLOVABLE,
PART ONE

Birth can be hazardous to your health.

There we are, in a warm and blissful environment, all our wants and needs fulfilled instantly, when suddenly the worst disaster film of all time begins to roll. The walls shudder and contract, we start down a long, dark tunnel toward an uncertain end, only to be yanked out, upended, snipped, spanked, and forced to breathe the cold air of an alien world. And that is if we have an easy birth. It is possible, for example, to spend all day stuck in the tunnel or to experience one of the dozens of other complications of the birth process.

While we cannot go back and get birthed again, we can look at any decision our minds made at the time to see if any of those decisions are affecting us now. An example of a birth decision is, "Just when things are going fine, the bottom will always drop out." Naturally, if we believe that this is the case, our lives will go precisely according to that formula. One of the central tasks of life is spotting the decisions and beliefs that are causing our lives to unfold in their particular ways. Once spotted, these beliefs and decisions can evaporate or be replaced by healthier beliefs.

HOW WE COME TO FEEL UNLOVABLE,
PART TWO

Somewhere along the line many of us reach a conclusion about ourselves: something is wrong with me. I remember looking around me one day as a child and thinking, Either these people are crazy or I am. Fortunately for me, I decided it was them. But there was always the nagging suspicion that it might be me.

So many things in the growing up process can trigger an "I'm unlovable" decision that it is difficult to know where to begin. Let's consider the worst first.

All too many of us are born into an environment where we are not loved. This might not apply to you, but even if it doesn't I would like you'd consider the problem for a moment.

It is still common for children to be born into situations where they are unwanted. Mother Teresa of Calcutta speaks of children that she and her associates pick off garbage dumps where they have been left. For every child that is abandoned because it is unloved, there are doubtlessly hundreds that are kept by their parents to be raised in a hostile environment. If these impressionable minds are exposed to unloving words, deeds, and gestures on the part of those around them, they are likely to conclude that they are unlovable.

TAKING IT PERSONALLY

One awesome yet understandable error that growing humans make is to take personally the events that befall them. In my own case, I grew to feel that I was a burden upon my mother, because I always saw her rushing around in a harried manner in an attempt to get to work on time, get dinner ready, straighten up the house. It looked to me like I was the cause of all this bustle, that if I had not been there things would go more smoothly. I checked this out with my older brother, who for his own reasons assured me that this was indeed the case.

My big mistake, though, was taking this situation personally instead of seeing that the same would have been true no matter who the child was. So too it goes with children who are born into unloving environments. For good reason they take it personally, because they are unable to separate out what is happening to them from what would be happening if someone else were there instead. If guardian angels were more active on our planet, I would like one of their functions to be whispering in our ears in times of stress, "Don't take this personally. This would be happening even if somebody else were here instead of you."

Even if we are born into a generally loving environment, our sensitive eyes and ears pick up the negative feelings our parents have mixed in with their love. Parents often have anger, fear, sadness, unfulfilled wants, and other feelings mixed in with their positive feelings toward their children. We sense these largely unspoken feelings and suspect that we are the cause of them.

I have spent some time trying to find out what some of those negative feelings were at my own birth and in my early life. One of these feelings was fear. Certainly my mother had a number of survival-related fears. The bottom had just dropped out of her world. My father died while she was pregnant with me, forcing her to change roles in midlife. One week she was a happy housewife with a growing family, the next week a widow with one and one-half children to support. If babies can sense their parents' feelings by osmosis, as many psychologists now think, I must have picked up a heavy dose of fear. I was born into a classic case of mixed feelings. My mother wanted me (she had formed a goal early in her married life of having six redheaded boys), and at the same time she didn't want me (my presence was a complicating factor in a time of grief and economic worry). Naturally I was not able to figure out all that at the time; all I knew was that something was wrong. There seemed to be some secret I didn't know, a missing piece to the puzzle. So I decided that it must be that I really was not welcome, that I was being put up with grudgingly. I also knew at the same time that I was welcome-what an odd paradox! People fed me and were generally kind, but there were all those sighs and whispered conversations between my grandmother and mother. "What on earth am I going to do?" I overheard my mother say one day. Was I the focus of all this? I was afraid to ask for fear of finding out that I was. I kept out of the way and became a good boy.

HOW WE COME TO FEEL UNLOVABLE,
PART THREE

Birth and the early days of life are full of opportunities to forget that we are unlovable. As we grow, though, particularly through talking and listening to the people around us, it gets even easier to forget to love ourselves. One of the biggest problems a child has is that almost everyone you *meet* will try to talk you out of your own experience. When you feel scared they will say "There's nothing to be scared of," and when you are sad they will say "Don't cry." When we feel joy we hear "Calm down." Their intentions are usually good, but the effects are hard on us because we are led further away from our own experience. The implication for us is that there is something wrong with our experience: fear, sadness, joy are things to be rid of rather than opened up to and embraced. Of course we can see now that our parents and others were trying to keep us from feeling bad-largely because when we feel bad, they feel bad too.

Once we lose touch with our own experience we start looking around outside ourselves to see what we can do that works in our particular setting. This leads us to adopt a set of actions that are designed largely to please others. There's no problem with pleasing others unless we do so at the expense of our own experience, and unfortunately for us that is usually what we do. Being me doesn't work, we think, so what must I do to get my needs met here?

Whatever works! For some of us it works to be a Good Boy or Good Girl. For others it works to be a Holy Terror. Another adopts the mask of Shy Kid, while still others play Bully. There are thousands of different personas that we adopt to get some recognition as we grow. The Latin word *persona* means "mask." It is the root of our own word *personality. In* our search for what works, we build up a personality based on masks we don to get recognition. But that's not all. Another part of the personality comes from those things we do to avoid the pain of not getting our needs met.

Recall that I became a Good Boy to please my mother and stay out of her way as much as possible. One day I was running my Good Boy act in high gear when disaster struck. I had overheard my mother telling my grandmother how much she wanted to have the bathroom redecorated. I filed this away in my six-year-old mind, and one afternoon after school I went to work. My brother, who was supposed to be watching me, went up the street to play with a friend (my brother later paid dearly for this slip in vigilance). I got out my crayons, finger paints, and watercolors and painted a fantastic mural all over the bathroom walls. It was an intricate assortment of camels, pyramids, Disney characters, and scenes from Robin Hood. I heard the crunch of my mother's tires in the driveway and ran out excitedly to bring her in to see. I remember dragging her down the hall and proudly flinging open the bathroom door. Instead of being pleased, she exploded, and so did my carefully constructed eager-to-please persona. I got the spanking of my young life.

So one day the persona stops working, seemingly for no reason, and we put aside the question, What can I do to please these people? replacing it with a negative question, What can I do to avoid pain while getting some recognition? The first question was largely positive answers, the second question only negative. There are many ways to avoid pain.

> Withdraw into yourself-don't let anybody know who you
>   are. Don't play the game.
> Mess up the game so nobody can win.
> Become a problem kid.

These methods are not designed to make you a winner-you've already decided you will never be able to win. They are designed to keep you from losing completely. Even negative recognition is better than none at all.

HOW WE COME TO FEEL UNLOVABLE, PARTS FOUR THROUGH INFINITY

If birth and early life decisions do not cause you to forget to love yourself, then the estrangement from your own experience, which we discussed above, often will. Following these events, we are often subject to a barrage of other life experiences that seem to be designed to convince us we are unlovable.

For example, our parents have expectations for us. They want us to be smart or successful or to do something they never had a chance to do. Usually these expectations are unspoken, so that we have to puzzle them out for ourselves. There are two major problems with expectations. First, we are often unable to meet them, and therefore feel unlovable when we fall short. Second, we sometimes meet the expectations. We often arrive at a goal and think, I should be happy now. But we are not, not for long anyway. For the fact seems to be that when we meet a goal that is not one of our own free choosing, we experience a sense of emptiness. We have looked outside ourselves for someone else to set a goal, for someone else to approve of us, and in so doing we have lost touch with our inner sense of what we want and what it takes to feel satisfied.

Too often also we come to associate love with things. We feel sad, so we buy some clothing to make us feel better. We feel inadequate, so we jack up our sense of self with a sports car. These things work for a moment, but the temporary high wears off and we are back to dissatisfaction again until we find a new antidote.

THE TABOO AGAINST LOVING YOURSELF

I am a psychologist and concern myself mainly with transformation in individuals and small groups. It pleases me, though, to see how someone has taken some of these basic ideas and put them in a historical perspective. John Crosby, in a brilliant article that deserves wide attention, has examined the origin of the taboo against loving ourselves. (*John Crosby, "On the origin of the taboo against self-love," *The* Humanist, Nov./ Dec. 1979, pp. 45-47.)

Crosby observes that the reason we do not love ourselves is not so much that we do not know how but that we have a belief that it is wrong to have self-esteem. He traces this belief through Western culture back to certain parts of the Bible in which an idol was defined as anything that could claim the allegiance and loyalty of the human heart. To prevent people from elevating the self to a position rivaling that of God, the early church fathers began to characterize the self as unclean,. sinful, in need of redemption. The self was off to a bad start in every possible way.

What is the basis for this attitude? Dr. Crosby points out that there are two accounts of creation in Genesis. The one in the first chapter is dramatically different from that in the second chapter.

The View in *Chapter* One	The View in *Chapter Two*
God is humanistic.	God is authoritarian.
Creation is a good thing.	Creation is a test for Adam and Eve.
God is egalitarian.	God is patriarchal and uses woman as an agent for Adam's sin.
God makes man and woman his own image.	No image mentioned, only in punishment for transgression.

We can only guess at the reasons the early church fathers made the second creation story the cornerstone of Christian dogma. First, they probably did not feel very good about themselves. It would be difficult for someone who felt good to embrace such a bleak view of the human condition. Second, if one were interested in building up a strong church, one would find it an advantage to have constituents who felt in strong need of redemption. If people can be led to believe that they are sunk deep in sin and that the church is the means of redemption, a prosperous future for the church is virtually assured. Recall also that these were rough, often savage times, when a benign version of the human condition would be hard to support. For these and other reasons Western culture was built upon the foundation of a remarkably negative view of the self. Subsequent religious movements, such as the Protestant Reformation of Luther, Puritanism, and the Methodist movement of Wesley, sought to get back to an even bleaker view of ourselves. Catholic or Protestant, the view was the same: man is a depraved sinner in need of redemption.

With such a negative view in circulation for the past two thousand years, we must give ourselves credit for even entertaining the idea of loving ourselves.

GETTING FREE

All these things we have learned. We see the world exactly upside down. Our task is to set our vision straight again. Let's see if we can identify some basic attitudes that will set us free.

I have learned to see the world the way it isn't.

I have done this for my survival.

I am now interested in much more than survival.

I can see it the way it is.

There is nothing outside myself that can save me.

I have everything I need inside me.

All the love I have been searching for is here within me.

I demand it from others because I am unwilling to give it to myself. I can give it to myself.

My very nature is love, so there is no need to search for it, no need to work at it.

Love is the only thing I need to change.

I commit to loving myself as much as I can...always...all ways.

CHAPTER THREE
How To Do It

I think I can be most helpful by writing about how I go about loving myself rather than offering instructions on how you can do it. In that way I can get down into my own consciousness, into my own experience of loving myself, so that the territory we can explore will be uncharted and exciting for us both. At the end of the chapter, though, I will make a list of instructions so they can be easily remembered.

At the moment I write this I am aware that fate has served up a perfect experience for me to work on. Today I have a sore throat. That may seem trivial, but to me it's a big deal because I *hate* being sick. So, on the day I want to write about the experience of loving myself, I come up with something I hate. Perfect.

Logically I know there is nothing wrong with being sick. Everybody gets sick. But being sick feels to me like some kind of cosmic setback. If I were *really* on top of things in myself, I wouldn't get sick. I would head things off before I actually succumbed. Then, too, there is this infernal theory that I and many others hold that there is a direct relationship between mind and body, that the body gets sick because I have some need to get sick to work out an issue in the mind. It is a valid theory from a scientific standpoint: there are hundreds of studies linking states of mind and emotion with diseases from headache to cancer. Believing this theory inspires me to take good care of myself. Since I started seeing things this way I have stopped smoking, lost weight, and started meditating and exercising regularly. Before, when I was a smoker, an overeater, and a worrier, I got sick frequently. I had three or four colds a year, plus an assortment of influenzas and digestive upsets. Now, for the past eight years, I have been remarkably free of illness. In this eight-year period I can recall two colds, two flus, and one stomach upset, the latter of which I can forgive because I was falling in love at the time.

So I think my life is much healthier by believing the body-mind theory, but the problem comes when I actually get sick. Then I can't just be sick like the next guy. I have to puzzle over it, see where I let down my guard, and generally make myself wrong for having done it to myself. That is what I am doing at the moment. Let me see, though, if I can give myself a clear experience of loving myself for it anyway. I pause and close my eyes.

Ah, I see what must be done. Where I am at the moment is hating myself for being sick. So that is what needs to be loved first. *Love whatever you can from wherever you are.* Let me see if I can do that. I say in my mind, I love myself for hating myself for being sick. I feel a wave of light and lightness pass through my body. I am very aware of the pain in my throat, as if someone has turned a spotlight on it.

My mind skips off to another subject: trying to figure out how and why I gave myself a sore throat. It's in the throat, so maybe it is because I have held back on some important feelings or communications. Perhaps something is going on that I can't swallow.

Here's a paradox.

One of the hardest things about learning to love yourself is to remember that all you have to do is love yourself for how you are feeling at the moment. Yet this is also the thing that makes loving yourself totally effortless. All you have to do is catch the way you actually are and love it. So I was feeling like I hated myself, and that was the very thing that needed to be loved. I couldn't love myself for having a sore throat until I could love myself for hating myself for having a sore throat.

Now my mind comes back to the task at hand, and I love myself again. This time I feel a sweet warmth in my chest. I let It expand and with a full deep inhalation the feeling spreads throughout my body.

Now I would like to love myself directly for having a sore throat. I let myself experience that, and my head feels like it nearly explodes with light. For some reason today my experience of loving myself is full of light. Now I feel a sense of peace spreading over my body and mind, as if the work is done for now.

LATER SATURDAY

My experience of loving myself is physical. I may start the Idea in my mind, but I feel it connect and happen in my body. It feels like an expansion. I feel an expansion of space when I love myself.

Love is being in the same space with something. Perhaps I am sad. If I'm not able to share space with it, I will try to talk myself out of it. When I am able to love it, though, it feels like I am opening space around the sadness, allowing it to be.

Love gives space, makes room. If I dislike someone, for example, it would be unloving to crowd out that feeling before I have inquired into it. First, I need to love it the way it is. Not to love the person, but to love myself for disliking him. This action makes room for me to be the way I am. It aligns me with what is actually going on. It allows me to inquire into why I do not like the person rather than thinking *I should* like him. Then perhaps I will come to the position of loving my neighbor, but supported by a foundation of loving myself.

MONDAY MORNING

The start of a week, and I have a thousand things to do. Today I need to go to the bank and the post office. I have a number of letters waiting to be written-and not the kind I can leisurely put off. Then I must see several therapy clients in the afternoon. All this and a book to write. I guess I feel harried. I close my eyes and settle back into my chair for a moment. What is this feeling of harriedness? Can I learn to love it? I search inside and find that there is a tight, antsy feeling in my chest along with a bunch of thoughts tumbling through my mind. One thought reminds me of an errand I must do, another mournfully observes that I will never get everything done.

I soften and relax into the tight, antsy feeling in my chest. I feel a wave of bliss pass through that part of my body; I suddenly feel much more cheerful. I find myself smiling. Something relaxes down in my stomach. I say in my mind, I love myself for feeling harried, and my body smiles back.

MONDAY *AFTERNOON*

I realize that there is nothing that really needs to be done in learning to love ourselves other than to be willing to love ourselves. We have spent so many years being unwilling to love ourselves that to simply turn it around and be willing to love sets in motion a tide of energy that will carry us along.

It goes back to that basic decision we make: to experience or not to experience. Are we going to allow ourselves to taste life directly, or do we rely on what others have tasted? There are advantages to relying on others' experience of life. It is safer, and you do not have to learn the rules for yourself. You do not have to feel as much pain. The trouble is that you do not get to feel joy, either. There's no passion for those who stay one step removed.

A major turnaround point in our lives comes when we become willing to experience. Then we can begin to feel joy and passion. We can also begin to take some responsibility for our own lives. When we are still relying on other people's experience (parents, church, friends), we always have them to blame when things go wrong. We also cannot take credit when things go right.

I think we take a basic willing or unwilling stance in our bodies and minds, even though, once we turn the corner and become willing to experience, we still must go through thousands of little decisions about whether we are willing to experience a particular thing. The big decision to be willing sets us free to begin the journey to our center. It gives us energy and passion. Then, at each step along the way, we have the opportunity to open a little more, to become a bit more willing. Then, on occasion, a sweet and potent reward will come our way. Like the one I experienced a few hours ago.

I had just meditated for a half-hour or so, and I was resting for a few minutes in a reclining position to enjoy that clear and peaceful post-meditation state of mind. I decided to open myself to any feelings I had been unwilling to experience recently. As soon as I made that decision, some sorrow and loss drifted through. I was missing my daughter, in camp on the other side of the country. I experienced those feelings for a moment, and they passed on. After a moment of quiet I began to feel an exhilaration in my body, accompanied by a deep sense of gratitude for everything that I experienced, all of life. I felt wave after wave of bliss cascade through my body. Along with the bliss came a shivering vibration, as if my body was dancing internally with the joy of life itself. In a few moments this feeling subsided, and I felt peaceful and relaxed again. These moments, like a deep and passionate embrace with the universe, give my life richer meaning.

TUESDAY MORNING

The notion of loving myself is coming in dimly this morning, like a beacon through the fog. I am thinking that love is the same thing as accepting the truth. When I have something about myself I have not loved, it is like a truth I have not accepted fully. For example, suppose I am scared of failing. If I haven't accepted the truth of that fear and loved it the way it is, I am either indifferent to it or I have denied it. In any case I am at the mercy of it. When I become willing to experience the truth of it, I invite it out of the shadows into the light. I become willing to share space with it. I allow it to be. Since it already existed anyway, all I have changed is my willingness to experience it. That tiny shift makes all the difference in the world, though. When I am unwilling to experience something, I am dense and contracted. When I become willing to experience it, I open and expand. All that has been changed is that I have dropped my resistance to experiencing it. When I find myself dense and contracted, I often ask myself, What is the truth that I am trying to withdraw from in this situation? Tension is the energy it takes to keep truth out of our awareness.

LATER TUESDAY MORNING

I see that another block to loving ourselves is our beliefs about how good we should feel. Loving myself feels very, very good. A moment ago I leaned.back in my chair and loved myself deeply, feeling that warm rush of acceptance through my body and mind. But then I reached a place where I would not let myself feel anymore, and I skipped off into some worry thoughts. What is it that keeps me from letting myself feel good?

I remember seeing a lot of grim faces around me as a child; I think I wondered if that was the way I was supposed to be. Perhaps I put an upper limit on my ability to let myself feel good so that I would not rock the boat in my family. Too, I remember that people frequently had to caution me not to get excited, because I was always bubbling over with enthusiasm for a new idea or a new toy. I, remember when I got hold of the Idea of God for the first time, perhaps when I was six or seven.. I nearly drove the adults in my world mad with questions and speculations on the subject. Then, when my grandfather gave me a new basketball for my birthday, I carried it everywhere, even to sleep with me at night. Even at this moment I can remember the sweet, dark leathery smell of that ball next to me on the pillow. I was forever being restrained, usually for my own good, but probably often for the sake of those around me, so as not to raise the emotional tone beyond a certain comfort point. I suspect that eventually I installed my own governor inside me, a restraint to keep myself from feeling so good that it threatened those around me. Now, when I open up to love and expand into space, I run up against those restraints imposed by myself long ago. Let me see if I can release them now that I no longer need them.

I lean back in my chair and say to myself, It's all right to feel as good as I can. In my consciousness it immediately feels like the bottom drops out and the lid pops off! I feel bursts of joy, like Roman candles, firing from the bottom of my body to the top. A picture leaps into my mind of Moses coming down from the mountain thousands of years ago with a vastly different set of commandments. "I have news for you," he says. "There is no limit to how good you can feel." What a difference that might have made in our history!

I feel relaxed, comfortable, safe. The only true safety is being willing to expand beyond our limits.

The very thing I get stuck on is always the very thing I need to learn to love. I will beat my head against something again and again until I finally get the message: It's there because I haven't learned to love it. Whatever is there is there to be loved. And it will gladly wait around a few minutes or a few decades until I learn to love it. Now that I open up to it, I see that the anger I spoke of a moment ago has been there for years. It goes back five years with the woman I spoke of, but I can feel that it is the same kind of anger I have felt a thousand times before-with friends, parents, lovers. It is a helpless feeling of knowing that I am not going to get what I need and want in the situation. I expand to embrace my anger, that steamy feeling that makes my head hot, and it eventually dissolves into light.

LATER

Love makes life very simple. If we take seriously the idea that love is the only thing that needs to be changed in any situation, life can become quite simple. Life becomes a series of opportunities to learn to love more. We need not concern ourselves with matters like wrong and right because the only thing that is important is how much love we are expressing through our actions. Only we can determine that for ourselves, and there is no need to defend ourselves if we find that little love is being expressed through our actions. That fact becomes the very thing we need to love. Life is learning to love.

WEDNESDAY MORNING

The mistake I see myself and other people making with regard to loving ourselves is treating love as an intellectual exercise, as something we should do. I think this stems from our inability to see that it is something we can do effortlessly. All we need to do is love ourselves for whatever we are feeling. If we feel dislike toward someone, we can love ourselves for disliking him or her. If we cannot love ourselves at the moment, we can love ourselves for not being able to love ourselves. Our mistake is thinking that we have to change something before we can love ourselves. The truth is that love is the only thing that needs to be changed. You don't have to get better before you can love yourself.

Often the main lesson of a journey is: Go back where you started and learn to love it all. Even though we may travel around the earth, we still take the unloved parts of ourselves with us. There will come a time when we wake up and realize that we must open up to those unloved parts, that if we do not make friends with them, no journey will feel satisfying. Once we become willing to share space with the unloved aspects of ourselves, any journey, even a walk around the block, has meaning.

These have been some thoughts and experiences of mine over a few days of my life. The reader will find instructions embedded in the actual moment of loving myself, but for those, like me, who like to see their how-to-do-it instructions spelled out in a 1-2-3 format, try these as experiments.

1. Notice your present state of mind or feeling. It could be mad, scared, joyous, hating yourself, bored, neutral.
2. Love yourself for what you are experiencing. It matters not if you do not know how to love yourself. At first just say the words if you can't figure out how. Say

"I love myself for (not being able to love myself, being scared, feeling happy, etc.)."
After a while you will probably identify a physical sensation of loving yourself.

3. Stay with it as long as it feels interesting and comfortable.

4. Remember, you don't need to go around loving yourself all the time for your life to work wonderfully. You just have to go around being willing to love yourself. Willingness lets you flow with the stream rather than against it.

WHAT IS EXPERIENCE AND WHAT IS NOT

In learning to love ourselves, it is the experience of loving ourselves that has the power to change everything. It will serve us, then, to find out just what experience is, so that we will not waste time in the frustrating world of non-experience.

When I am interested in deeply understanding a word, I start with the dictionary. As a noun, the first definition tells us that *experience* is "the act of living through an event or events; personal involvement in or observation of events as they occur." That actually tells us a great deal. It means, for example, that non-experience is not actually living through an event Experience is what we have observed or undergone personally.

The dictionary goes on to say that experience is anything observed or lived through, as to say one's trip was a pleasant experience. As a verb, to experience is to undergo, to feel, to meet with, to encounter.

What are some of the popular modes of non-experience? In other words, how do we keep ourselves from actually experiencing life?

BELIEF

Belief is one type of non-experience that traps us. Believing in loving yourself, for example, is a position the mind takes when it is unable to have the experience of loving itself. Or, perhaps, you have once had the experience of loving yourself and are now attempting to get back to that space again. If one has a strong experience of, say, enlightenment while standing under an apple tree, one may come back time and again to hang around apple trees. But in the experience of loving ourselves, now is the moment that counts, and it does us little good to try to get back to the way things were when the idea first took us by surprise.

Once a person who had trekked to India in search of truth was meditating in his guru's garden when he experienced a blinding flash of light and a rush of pure energy. "I've found God," he exclaimed to his guru. The guru nodded. "Yes, you found God." So the man went excitedly back to meditating in the garden, but after two weeks had not experienced any more flashes of light or rushes of energy. He went dejectedly back to his guru and asked what the problem was. "You found God while meditating in the garden," the guru said. "Don't go looking for Him there anymore."

Clearly, belief is a poor substitute for experience. It seems to tide us over until we can have a certain experience, but ultimately we seem to be required to let go of the belief in order to have the actual experience. A woman I know told me that all her life she believed she would meet the man of her dreams. From earliest recollection, her favorite stories had been those with a Prince Charming who came along and took the princess away to a happy life. As an adult she had one unsatisfactory love affair, after another until she woke up one day to what she was doing. She realized she would fall in love with men who swept her off her feet but would lose interest when flaws in them began to emerge. She saw that she was replaying her childhood fairy tales as an adult. She had a belief in a special sort of love which had to be accompanied by a special sort of behavior in the man; when these expectations were not met, she became dissatisfied with him. Her beliefs were keeping her from having the actual experience. She became willing to give up the beliefs, and when she did, it did not take long until she began a much more satisfying relationship with a man she had previously dropped. This person's experience is very common; I have seen hundreds of examples in therapy when people have let go of certain limiting beliefs, often adopted in childhood, and experienced profound changes in their lives.

DECIDING

Deciding to love yourself is another poor substitute for the actual experience of it. Deciding works well in matters of choice: smooth or crunchy peanut butter? Right or left at the corner? Bach or Beatles on the stereo? Fortunately for us, there is no choice about loving ourselves. We must do it for life to work. So, a decision to love yourself, while it may point the way toward the experience of it, is not the actual experience. Decisions are to deal with mind-stuff; loving yourself is heart stuff, and goes beyond the mind's limits.

HOPING

Hoping is another mode of non-experience. It is common for us to hope something will be different; the very act of hoping, which keeps us from experiencing it deeply the way it is, traps us in the realm of non-experience.

Hoping that something will be different practically guarantees that it will not change: One of the fundamental laws of change seems to be that things need space in order to change. They need room around them in order to find a new form. So, for example, if you wish to change your feeling of depression into something more pleasant, you would not want to try to talk yourself out of it, tense against it, or take a pill to alleviate it. These approaches would deny space to the feeling; they would not give your depression any room. What would work (based on many experiences of working with depression over the years in my therapy practice) would be to allow the feeling to be. Don't turn your back on it, but release your tight grip on it so that it has moving space. We would want to explore it, feel it, inquire into it, taste it, dance with it. We would take a willing attitude toward it so we could learn what it is about.

Notions like hoping, believing, wishing, and deciding are based on fear. We feel afraid, for example, that we do not love ourselves, so we hope that we will. We feel afraid that we will stay depressed, so we wish or decide that it will be different. The trouble is that all of these approaches are space-denying: they do not acknowledge that the thing we are trying to change is lovable. They operate on the assumption that we are to be rid of the thing we are trying to change, rather than to open up to it.

THE BREAKTHROUGH

We make a profound breakthrough at the moment we drop notions like hoping and believing and start actually experiencing things. Let's say we are in despair. When we put our energy into hoping the despair will lift, it is likely to stay the way it is, because we will have no energy to explore it, see what it is about, accept the truth of it.

To accept it the way it is does not mean we listlessly give up. In fact, accepting it the way it is has tremendous power.

The first step in generating positive change is to see it clearly, whatever it is. That step puts us into the realm of experience. It also opens us to some higher awarenesses which are reserved for those who are willing to experience life directly.

Look at the following table, reading from the bottom up.

The Transition from Non experience to Experience

Experience 8. Being willing to be the *source* of love for yourself and others.

       7 Being willing to personally *experience* loving yourself.

      6. Accepting things the way they are (e.g., you don't love yourself, you have a lot of reasons why you don't love yourself, you are afraid of loving yourself).

Non- 5. Reasoning that you are lovable experience

      4. Believing that you should love yourself.

      3. Deciding you will love yourself.

      2. Wishing you could love yourself.

      1. *Hoping* you can love yourself.

Below the line is the realm of non-experience. The first act of getting above the line is to see things the way they are. In other words, to get out of the mud, one must first acknowledge that one is stuck in the mud. Hoping you are not stuck will not help, nor will wishing, believing, deciding, or being reasonable about it. To acknowledge that one is stuck in the mud has power, because it leads to other key questions. How stuck am I? How can I get out? Do I need help or can I do it myself? What can this experience teach me about living? It is an odd paradox that only by inquiry into the mud can we get to the light.

So much energy goes into pretending to ourselves and others that we are not stuck in the mud that we spin our wheels furiously, to the mud-spattered chagrin of the bystanders in our life.

Once we get above the line, life goes a little smoother. We feel more, we see more, we hear more. Of course, not all of it is pleasant, but at least it is real. After the years and decades we have spent in the illusory world of our hopes and beliefs, reality has a refreshing clarity and power to it, even if some of it is unpleasant.

"The surest test if a man be sane," says the Chinese Book of Tao, "is if he accepts life whole, as it is."

Accepting life whole, as it is, not only restores our sanity but also puts us in line for the higher experiences of life, such as the one listed at the top of the preceding table. A height in experience is to be willing to be the source of love for yourself and others. To be the source of love means that you are no longer striving for love: you are love. When you are fully open to love, you can provide an endless supply of it for yourself and others.

The gateway to the higher experiences of life seems to be the moment when we decide we are willing to see life the way it is. Being willing does not mean we have to see all the truth at once, nor could we. It is a simple shifting of our basic attitude toward life. Look more closely at the crossover point that separates experience from nonexperience. We have seen that taking things the way they are is the key move that catapults us into reality. The actual process by which we can do this is so gentle and subtle that it is positively lazy. It all hinges upon the notion of willingness.

To become willing to experience is all that is required. The act of becoming willing moves us out of the realm of illusion. To become willing to experience opens us up to what is actually happening. Willingness to experience the truth is the tiny adjustment that invites the truth. Willingness to feel is the act that dispels the fog of unconsciousness and allows us to come alive to our feelings. At the moment we become willing to experience what is real, we shed the dead weight of all our illusions. To become willing is to become free.

It seems easy. Why don't we do it more readily? Because to see life as it is involves dropping our resistance to pain. We would not have retreated into the world of illusion had we not experienced too much pain to handle some time earlier in life. Somewhere we learned to retreat from love into fear. And now to be free we must expand again into love, which for many of us means that we must go through a few layers of pain and fear. That is no fun. It is never fun to look out the window of your car and see that you are up to your hubs in mud. It must be done, though. The alternative, to shut your eyes and hope the mud will go away, only works for a while. Whenever the fragrance of a rose enchants us, we need to keep in mind that its roots, and the seeds from which it grew, are deep in the mud.

CHAPTER FOUR
Learning To Love Your Feelings

A man gets into an argument with his boss; later, that evening, he is still recycling angry thoughts through his mind. A high school teacher wants to rid himself of the sexual feelings he has for some of the girls in his classes. A young woman persistently feels scared in her interactions with men her own age. A sixty-year-old widow still struggles with grief over the death of her husband five years before.

These examples are a few that come to mind from my therapy practice over the past ten years. They are examples of the kinds of feelings with which normal people wrestle every day of their lives. Feelings are an important part of our lives. They make us feel alive. Yet at times they are so painful, so elusive, so difficult to handle. What attitude toward our feelings will allow us to transform them? What can we do to keep them from recycling? Can we keep the positive ones while deleting the negative? Can we actually learn to love our feelings, even the ones we hate? These are key questions to answer along the way to loving ourselves.

WHERE DO FEELINGS COME FROM?

As nearly as we can tell, certain basic feelings are automatic. That is, in certain situations humans will typically react with certain feelings. Here are several common situations which trigger predictable feelings.

Situation -	*Feeling*
Loss of a loved person, place, or thing (Examples: Death; divorce; moving)	Sadness, Grief, Sorrow
Not having a solution to the problem at hand (Examples: You are stuck in an elevator; a wild animal gets loose; your wife tells you she's leaving)	Fear, Anxiety
Unlikelihood of getting what you want or need (Examples: You realize that you will never get your parents' approval; your mother won't give you a cookie)	Anger; later, Depression
Likelihood of getting what you want or need (Examples: You are about to get your college degree; the day before vacation)	Excitement; later, Joy

So far so good. Events occur, and certain feelings arise. If it stopped here all would be well. We are more complex than that, however. We are so complex that we take something simple and normal like feelings and magnify them so that they can dominate our lives. Feelings get so big and real that we take pills to keep them at bay, drink to escape them, even kill ourselves because we cannot stand them.

How do these simple things get out of hand? In a word, resistance. Rather than opening up to our feelings and letting them pass through, we go solid around them, thus trapping them and giving them a permanent reality in our lives. An event occurs that triggers anger, for example. Instead of opening up to the anger, feeling it and letting it go, we instead resist it and hold on to it. Then we are stuck with holding on to the past while trying to deal with the present.

Recall that we have stacks of beliefs in our minds that we have picked up from parents, schooling, church, and society. We may have a belief that "big boys don't cry" or that "sexual feelings are bad." When these normal feelings arise in the body, the mind comes into play. The mind with its awesome cleverness can talk the body out of experiencing what it is experiencing. The body remembers, though, and feels a growing estrangement from the mind.

This is the process by which we get out of touch with our feelings. No wonder that they feel unlovable. They are strangers to us, and our first tendency is to mistrust strangers simply because we do not know them or perhaps because we fear they mean us harm. Let's look at several feelings separately.

GUILT

Guilt is a disabling feeling that holds us perpetually in check. It keeps us from truly enjoying ourselves. Guilt so permeates us at times that the most guilty among us do not even suspect that they are operating out of guilt. But what is guilt? How does it feel? Where did it come from, and what is its purpose?

Guilt feels like a perpetual holding back. It is a pall over the body and mind. One foot is on the accelerator and the other on the brake pedal. The unpleasant, heavy feeling of guilt comes from the tension between these two forces. I will go inside myself and listen, so that I can find out what these forces are.

One force is my energy. It is the spontaneous, creative part of me. I can feel it pulsating down inside of me. It snakes, roils, vibrates. It wants to roar up through me to seek, explore, find fresh outlets. It wants to play. What is the other force, the foot on the brake pedal?

The restraining force is my own resistance. I am applying the brakes. Perhaps my parents told me to resist, or my Sunday school teacher, but now it is my own mind that is in charge of my resistance. Why? I ask myself the question and listen for the answer.

Deep inside I hear a crying. It feels like the pain I've felt a thousand times when I surrendered to my creative energy and got burned, or hurt, or scolded. It is the pain of the time I told you about earlier in the book when I sought to create a mural on the bathroom wall.We surrender to the playful, dancing creative urge, and without the information we need to guide us, we discover pain and disapproval.

This problem is so widely known that we encounter it in myths. One of the most popular myths to come out of Western culture was the Fisher King myth, which later grew into the myth of the Holy Grail. In the story a young king is exploring in the forest. He is tired and hungry. He spots a salmon roasting over a fire in the woods. The aroma is so overwhelming that he grabs a piece of the fish and thrusts it impulsively into his mouth, only to be burned horribly by the too-hot meat. It does not take a great leap of the mind to discover the moral of the story so far. Fortunately the myth is more complicated than this. The king, back in his castle years later, is suffering a profound spiritual crisis. He is miserable, he has lost the will to live, the kingdom is falling apart; life is meaningless. Although he has forgotten the long-ago incident in the woods, he now feels good only when he is fishing. This part of the story says something quite important about human growth. Even though we have been burned and have lost touch with our inner creative energy, we feel compelled to keep looking. We only feel good if we are searching for that elusive, unnamable thing.

The myths vary, but in one major version a knight comes along who is able to help the king find the Holy Grail. It is easy, because all the while the Grail has been in the innermost room of the castle! The king learns to open up to the creative, inner energy again.

Listen again to a few of the important parts of the tale.

We taste the delicious dish and get burned. We forget how and why we ever found and lost touch with that delicious thing, but we feel good only when we are looking for it. And later, perhaps with some assistance, we find it in the deepest part of ourselves. Why, this is our story! We seek love and approval outside while being unwilling to open up to ourselves to see that our very inner nature is love. We fail to find it out there and lapse into despair. Later we wake up to find that we had inside ourselves what we were looking for all those years.

Creative energy expresses itself in many ways, but one way is through the feelings. Feelings dance through constantly: fear, guilt, anger, joy, grief, sexuality. These feelings are powerful; they feel out of control at times. They alarm us. In our naivete we turn to parents and other authorities for advice on how to deal with these feelings. Of course we often hear what not to do. Don't feel, tighten up, don't touch down there, big boys don't cry, go to your room.

The big human brain makes big generalizations. Ideally, we should treat each instance as separate. We should think, I must not paint bathroom walls without my mother's permission. But the big brain draws big conclusions. It decides, don't surrender to the creative urge. Don't paint. Don't do anything without your mother's approval. Later in adult life these early decisions become the very shackles we must overthrow in order to be free.

The very nature of life is to create. Evolution is always working. The creative energy wants to leap and twist, flash in the sun, spiral upward. The tug-of-war continues,. even long after we have resolved our childhood guilt. No matter how high we go, how creative we become, we will always be asking ourselves questions like How creative can I let myself be? How much of myself will I let myself become?

On the good days we hum with creativity. Things work, we feel good. On the bad days we bump along, one foot on the brakes, in thrall to old pain and the expectation of disapproval.

I imagine this explains why writers and artists are notoriously difficult to live with. They are riding the edge of the energy, working the territory where the wave meets the rock. It is rough country there, and their lives are testimony to its roughness. Each of us has that same energy inside. It is part of what makes us human. For most of us the energy is unlikely to express itself on canvas or in a symphony. But it is there all the same. It is the raw stuff of growth. When we are open to it we feel alive. It is exhilarating, we feel movement. Closed to it we feel humdrum. Instead of a joyful noise we stifle a contented belch.

I see only one way to be free of guilt. We must take a willing stance toward our creative energy. We must say yes to growth, yes to life. We must also take a willing stance to our pain. When we first turn on the tap of our creative energy, some rusty water is likely to flow out in the form of old emotional traumas. After a while the stream will clear, but we must be willing to ride out that first wave of pain.

As we begin to roll, it is good to know that we can go as fast or as slow as we want. If we are moving too slowly we can decide to go faster. Too fast, we can consciously decide to slow down. Before, when we had one foot on the brakes and the other on the accelerator, we were at the mercy of things because we were running scared from our pain and the power of our creative energy. When we drop that resistance and embrace ourselves deeply, a dramatic reversal occurs. We are now fully in charge.

ANOTHER ASPECT OF GUILT

During meditation one morning a memory came vaguely into my awareness like a mosquito. It hovered for a moment, then lit upon me and nipped. The little pain of it gave me another view of guilt.

The memory is of a time about fifteen years ago when I came very close to cheating some people in a business deal. Although it happened that I didn't actually carry out the act of cheating, I came close enough that it gave me a look at a part of me I did not like very much. I was in a very stuck place at the time-up to my back pockets in emotional pain-and I saw the extent to which my own personal pain could dull my sense of caring and charity for others.

Now that memory floats through, and with it I can feel the agony of that time in my life. I feel again the pain of being in a marriage with someone I did not like anymore, of being overweight and out of shape and having a job I hated. I was burning up inside with a desire to be creative, but nothing I did seemed to work. My relationships were shallow and largely meaningless. Most things I kept inside, and half of what I communicated was lies. I was stuck.

I see that part of guilt, then, is the nipping memories of the unfinished business of old relationships and events in our lives. All that old unfinished business:

Lies we told,
Things we needed to say and didn't,

Things we wanted and didn't ask for,
People we loved and didn't tell,
People we hurt and didn't say "I'm sorry" to.

All these things and more are stored in the mind, and if we do not make some sort of gesture to that part of us, if we keep it out of our awareness, the memory of all that unfinished business hangs over us like a dark cloud. What sort of gesture can help?

Clearly we cannot go back. Whatever must be done must be done right now. One thing we can do in the present is to acknowledge that we have a huge storehouse of unfinished business. This act of acknowledgment lightens us up considerably because it lets us stop pretending. Then we can also acknowledge the pain we felt at the time and still feel, because of all the things we could not be, all the mistakes we made, all the things we wanted for ourselves and others. In a word, we can forgive.

In those old days I was so tied up in my mind that I could not acknowledge all the signals I was getting from my body. My body was yelling at me, "I'm mad, I'm scared, I need help, I need love, I hurt." My mind was saying, "Nothing's wrong, you can handle it, toughen up." I was putting so much energy into being right that I could not listen to what was going on inside me. Now, in the present, I can acknowledge those old feelings. When I do there Is a loosening of tension; I can breathe more freely.

Another action we can take to clear up these guilts Is to talk about them with people, even the very people involved, if they are still available. Talking about old unfinished business helps clear it up and has been known to generate small miracles. A man I know found himself able to forgive his exwife one day many years after they had split up. He felt a wave of forgiveness after talking about their relationship with a friend. The next day his ex-wife called him from across the country to tell him that she had suddenly had the experience of forgiving him and releasing some old anger she'd had toward him for years.

GUILT IS A CONCOCTION

One reason guilt is difficult to love is that it really does not exist. Guilt is a concoction, a murky mixture made up of fear, anger, and thoughts.

Let's say that you are on your way home from a secret liaison with your lover. You know that your spouse expected you an hour ago. You feel guilty. Let's separate out some of the parts of the concoction to see what we have. First, fear. You are scared, perhaps, of getting caught. You may be scared of having to tell a lie to your spouse. Then, you also may feel anger. The anger comes from not being able to have everything you want free and clear. Then there is the assortment of thoughts that the mind holds in the situation: "I should do this," "I shouldn't do that." All of these parts swirl and mingle together in our consciousness to make the feeling we call guilt.

Knowing that guilt is a concoction can be helpful in trying to love our way through guilt. If we are having trouble loving ourselves for feeling guilty, we can try loving the separate parts of it. It may be easier to love yourself for feeling scared, for example, than it is to love yourself for feeling guilty.

FEAR AND ANGER

Fear is at the rock bottom of all the feelings that trouble us. What could be more numbing than our deepest fears? These are some of the big ones:

Fear of dying,
Fear that there isn't enough to go around,

Fear of going crazy,
Fear of our sexual energy, Fear of being alone, and
Fear of fear itself.

We think, If I let myself feel my fear, I would never stop trembling. There seems something bottomless about it. Perhaps it is because it does not have an expressive component like a sob or a tantrum, as with sadness and anger. All you can do with fear is feel it and say, "I'm scared."

Fear is a mobilization of energy to solve a problem. If a gorilla jumps through the window of our sitting room, we would feel scared. This would mobilize energy in our body to seek a solution. We would run or do battle with the gorilla. The trouble is that nowadays our problems are so much more complicated that they seem to have no straightforward solutions. We live in a world of complex social relationships. There is a difference between the fear of confronting a gorilla and the fear of telling your spouse you're having an affair. One situation has some fairly straightforward solutions: you run or you fight. But the other? We are not sure yet of quite how to go about dealing with the complex fears of the modern world. In the U.S. approximately 100 million prescriptions for tranquilizers are written every year. If we knew a better way of dealing with fear, we would not reach so quickly for the pill bottle.

Resistance to fear, not fear itself, is of course our major problem. When we open up to fear and allow ourselves to feel it deeply, we can learn from it. We can inquire into it, find the source of it. If we are not willing to do that, though, if we take a posture of resistance to it, then it remains a numbing, permanent presence in our lives.

The same process is true for anger. It is hard to give ourselves permission to feel anger. It is crippling if we do not. By resisting the feeling of anger, we perpetuate it in our lives.

In addition, we ensure that it will leak out in ways that are troublesome to ourselves and others. When we drop that stance of resistance, a new world of energy opens up to us. At the bottom of every feeling is a positive lesson to be learned. In the case of anger, the lessons are bountiful. In any anger situation there are things we want and need. The anger would not be present if we were getting our wants and needs met. Rather than resisting the anger, we can open up to it, get to the bottom of it, and find out what we want and need. The same is true for the anger of others. We could well learn to ask ourselves in the presence of others' anger, What do they want or need? By operating in this manner we turn the negative energy of anger into the positive energy of looking for constructive solutions.

SADNESS

We hide our grief behind a wall of beliefs. We believe things like:

My pain is insignificant compared to others'. I have no right to be sad.

My pain is so great that I could never touch it. I'll feel better tomorrow.

If I ever let myself really.feel my sadness, I'd never stop crying.

All these things we tell ourselves keep the sadness locked up inside us. We are afraid to open up to it, to really let go into it, for fear that we may get so deeply mired in it we may never get out. Of course, the opposite is true. Being unwilling to feel it deeply keeps it trapped inside us. Sadness, fully felt, passes quickly.

All we really need to do is acknowledge our sadness. All we really must do to be free of it is be willing to feel it. Perhaps we still think that if we become willing to feel it, we must go around sad the rest of our lives. Ten years of working with the feelings of many people in therapy has shown me something I never would have guessed: When people truly open themselves to a particular feeling, even deep grief or rage, the expression of that feeling, only lasts a few minutes. Further, they always feel good afterwards. People tell me they feel cleansed, whole, light. I have never seen anyone who did not feel better after becoming willing to feel something they had been holding back. It has been a miracle to me to see person after person become willing to feel, and by doing so to become free.

FEELINGS ABOUT PARENTS

Some of the most difficult feelings we have are those about our parents. In my work as a therapist I have encountered hundreds of people who were stuck because they had feelings about their parents they could not accept and resolve. Our inability to deal with feelings about parents seems to me to rest on one simple problem. We feel simultaneous positive and negative feelings toward them, and we think that we must feel either one way or the other.

It is normal to feel anger toward your parents. It is normal to feel scared of them. It is normal to feel hurt by some of the things they do and do not do. You also feel grateful to them, love them, and have a host of other positive feelings. The complicating factor is that parents often do not want you to feel negative feelings toward them and will do things to try to keep you from feeling mad, scared, or hurt toward them. Through these kinds of interactions you begin to believe there is something wrong with your negative feelings in general, but this belief does not stop you from having negative feelings. It simply drives them underground.

This becomes the essence of our problem in learning to love our feelings. We believe there is something wrong with them; they are unlovable. Of course the only way to deal with negative feelings is to love them. How do you love something that is basically unlovable? So it goes around and around in the mind. It stops either when we change the belief from "negative feelings are unlovable" to "negative feelings are lovable" or when we go ahead and love them regardless of our beliefs.

THE BIG LESSON

Feelings are here to stay. We will never be rid of them, nor would we want to be. Feelings are what give us the sense of aliveness. In addition there is a tremendous amount to learn from them. In fact, feelings are best regarded as roadside pointers toward lessons we need to learn on our path. Each time there is something we are really angry about or scared of, there is a powerful lesson to be learned. It is usually something that we have withdrawn from in the past that we are now getting the opportunity to embrace. So it goes with other feelings, too. They each point the way toward things we need to learn about ourselves or the world.

Feelings are a perfect way to learn the big lesson of life. Since they cycle through so often, they give us endless opportunities to let go of resistance and open up to embrace ourselves with love.

CHAPTER FIVE
Learning To Love Your Body
And Your Sexuality

There are thousands of reasons why you should not love your body, thousands more reasons why you should not love your sexuality. The whole development of Western culture has been in part based on not loving sexuality and the body. And are we going to come along and change all that? Of course. We had better start by taking a deep breath and loving ourselves for not loving our bodies and our sexuality. That is where most of us begin.

If you asked a group of people, as I have often done in workshops, what their particular reasons are for not loving their bodies and their sexuality, they would give some of these popular responses.

I'm too fat.
I'm too skinny.
My legs are funny-looking.
My hair is too oily. I had an abortion once.
My father molested me.
My mother called me her "ugly duckling."
I got caught masturbating and got punished for it.

These are all great reasons not to love yourself. They all made perfect sense at the time. An event happened (your father molested you), you had feelings about the event (disgust, fear, anger), and you made some decisions about yourself and life (my sexuality causes disgusting things to happen, I'd better hide it). But notice that the decisions are made only of mindstuff and can be changed effortlessly. I have seen people change their decisions about some of the worst events imaginable. It moves me so much when I see someone take a hideous life event, like being raped or being in a concentration camp, and completely transform the negative feelings and decisions they made at the time so they could let go of the experience and live in the present again.

LEARNING TO LOVE MY OWN BODY

For me, learning to love my own body has been a major, and often rocky, path in my life, while learning to love my sexuality has been much easier for me. Nobody had much that was constructive or useful to say about sexuality in my family, but at least they did not burden me with much negative information or programming, either. So I was able to develop my own views of my emerging sexuality. I saw that it was to be nurtured and enjoyed, and that is the attitude I kept toward it throughout my adolescence. My body, though, is another story.

I was very fat when I was a kid. At the end of my first year of life I weighed in in the top five percent of all babies. Looking back on it I see that feeding me was probably the best way they had of keeping me quiet, even when I was bellowing for other reasons. I suspect I learned something in that first year that was to plague me later: no matter how you're feeling, eating will make it better. Under normal conditions we eat to satisfy hunger; we deal with other feelings in other ways. If we learn to eat to deal with feelings other than hunger, we have two bad habits on our hands. One is that we are eating in response to inner signals other than hunger. The other is that we have learned a poor way to deal with the other feelings. The result of both habits is the same: fat.

To make matters worse, I had a genetic problem to contend with. My father was "heavy" (translation: fat), and I resembled him in many ways. My mother and brother, the slender half of the family, took after each other.

How I hated being a fat kid! There is hardly anything worse than standing at the bottom of a tree that your friends are up in and being unable to climb it. I can still feel that pain today.

I hated my body and wrestled with it like an enemy for years. When I was in ninth grade I saw a weight specialist in a neighboring state who put me on a regimen of pills and diet that took seventy-five pounds off me in six months. I also went from being a C student to getting straight A's that year, assisted in part by the diet pills I took every day. They jazzed me up so much that I studied all the time because I could not get to sleep.* Later a coach helped me discover my body, and by the end of high school I was playing sports in an enthusiastic if undistinguished way.

It was still a wrestling match, though, because I had not resolved my fundamental problems with my body. No matter what it looked like on the outside, I still felt the same inside. The struggle continued until my late twenties, when I had the breakthrough experience I described in chapter one. I was finally able to love my body as it was. Before I could do that, though, I had to give myself permission to hate my body as much as I did. Then it became possible to love it.

Try an experiment with me. I am going to close my eyes and say "I love my body" several times in my mind. I will pause for ten seconds or so after each time to see and feel what happens in my body and mind. If you would be willing to do the same, perhaps we could compare the results.

*Note: I do not recommend this path to academic achievement. When they took me off the diet pills I crashed for two months until I could regain my natural equilibrium.

The first time I say it I feel a pleasant smiling sensation down in my stomach. Then my throat tightens up, so I open up to explore that tension. Memories appear in my mind about my days as a fat kid. I feel the pain of it, all the unspoken words and uncried tears.

Next time I say "I love my body" I get a strong wave of vibration that runs through me. It feels like a blast of pure energy. I wonder where that comes from.

Again I say "I love my body." I feel a deep satisfaction. I feel like I can accept even the part of me that still hates me. That is part of me, too. Even that is lovable:

Now a torrent of other feelings wells up. I feel sad, powerful, joyful. I feel myself wishing well to one or two people in my life who are away from me. I feel very alive. All this comes from being willing to love my body and everything in It.

What comes up for you? If you are like most of us, your first layer of experience is that layer of things you do not love about yourself. That is why I often say that learning to love yourself starts with learning to accept all the unloving feelings you have about yourself. But that's fine, because to love them is to replace the negative feelings with the positive feeling of love.

For many of us the body is the place we act out the self-destructive part of ourselves. When we are tuned in to the self-destructive programs in our minds, we do things like smoke, bite fingernails, have accidents, and poison ourselves in various ways. Whenever we are tuned in to those programs, often the very last thing that will occur to us is to love ourselves. Of course, loving ourselves is the quick ticket out of that unloving space.

In the final analysis, there are so many things we do not love about our bodies that the only sensible thing to do is to go ahead and love them anyway, regardless of how fat or skinny, how ugly or beautiful they are. Then, coming from a basic position of love, we can watch them change in directions we like, secure in the knowledge that it doesn't have anything to do with our basic lovability.

SEXUALITY

I would like to share some of my own views and experiences with regard to sex. So much has been written and spoken in our time about sexuality that it is not difficult to get lost in a fog of words. I would like to see if we can find our way through to see clearly what the essential issues are.

Our big problem with sexuality is that we have falsely learned that there is something wrong with sexual feelings. By believing that sexual feelings are something to be feared and restrained, we create for ourselves a poor relationship not only with our sexuality but with life itself. Where do these beliefs come from? Parents and society, often with the best of intentions, give us false information that causes us to estrange ourselves from our sexuality. It works like this. When sexual feelings are awakening in young people, their elders sense them. They stir up in the adults all their own issues with regard to sexuality. Parents want their children to avoid the pain of the mistakes they themselves have made. So the elders teach the children about sexuality, by words, gestures, or words not said. What they teach often has a major distortion: it confuses sexual feelings with sexual expression.

Ideally, we should teach children that sexual feelings are fine. They are a natural part of life, a deep source of energy and potential joy. We should teach them to be smart, though, about the expression of those feelings. We would teach them the advantages and disadvantages of the various aspects of sexual expression: masturbation, intercourse, flirting, and so forth. We should assist them in learning to open up to the feelings while finding means of expression that have positive consequences for all concerned.

Too often the elders confuse feelings with expression. We are taught that the feelings themselves are somehow wrong. This belief causes a logjam inside us. We have a deep sense that sexual feelings are good, overlaid by a belief that they are bad. This distortion causes us then to express our feelings in distorted ways.

To complicate matters, we also have a stack of decisions about sexuality based on old unpleasant events. I remember getting caught by my mother in the act of looking at some pictures of naked women. Several of my friends and I were studying these pictures, bought in the locker room from an eighth-grade entrepreneur, when my mother showed up unexpectedly. I remember the hot feeling of shame that swept over me when I saw my mother's reaction of anger and disgust. I saw in that moment that my sexuality was something she did not want to acknowledge, that somehow it made her uncomfortable. In fact, I never recall her or anybody in my family saying a word about sexuality in any way during my growing up. In a way I feel grateful, because at least I did not get a lot of distorted information that I later had to unlearn, but I feel wistful about not learning things about my sexuality that would have helped me feel more comfortable with myself.

Some of us have had much more unpleasant experiences with regard to sex than the mild event I just described. We have witnessed ugly scenes, been forced to have sex against our will, been seduced into doing things that we would not have done had we had our wits about us. We cannot change events, but we can always look for any decisions about ourselves or life that we made at the time. By looking at old decisions made in the heat of unpleasant experiences, we can break the grip the past has on us.

Beyond the traumas and the negative messages about sex is the fact that we often do not get any constructive information about it. We are not usually blessed with a guardian angel who can come along when we need it and say, "Sexual feelings are good. Let yourself feel them deeply. Surrender to them. Express them in ways that will bring happiness to all concerned." Adult life is a process of becoming a guardian angel to ourselves. We have to learn how to nurture ourselves and how to gather the kind of people around us that can nurture us in the ways we like.

We can begin by loving ourselves for all the reasons we do not love our sexuality, then going on through to open up in love and acceptance for those deeply positive sexual feelings inside. By learning how to love sexuality, we can learn more about how to love life itself, for sexuality is but one expression of a deeper life energy which resides in us all.

CHAPTER SIX
Clearing Your Mind

Many of our problems come from believing that there is an inadequate supply of love in the world. This delusion causes us to struggle for our share, or worse, to give up the struggle entirely. Part of learning to love yourself involves undergoing a radical transformation of how your mind sees things, so that you can see the world as a place where you are in total control of how much love you are willing to experience.

If you are willing to make that change of mind, let us look for a moment at the way the mind works. The mind is wired up to do many things, but one of its major functions is to have experiences and to make decisions based on those experiences. Usually this capability works well for us. We burn a finger on a hot stove, and the mind makes a useful decision based on that experience: "In the future I will not put my finger on hot stoves." However, unless we keep an eye on it, the mind will go further into troublesome territory. The mind will make general rules on how to live based on isolated past experiences. You will have an experience, like being slapped by your father, and the mind will make a generalization based on this experience that says, "You must be wary around large men." The mind, then, can take an experience (even a sentence, a glance, or a gesture) and take a point of view based on that experience. It will then treat similar experiences in the future on the basis of that past point of view. To put it another way, we experience an event and decide "that's how things are" rather than "that's how things were." We settle into positions about certain things and begin to act from those positions. The problem: each position we take decreases our freedom.

Some of the events that occur in our lives are extremely painful. From those events a heavy, rigid point of view can emerge. The painful experience which we need to consider here is the one (or thousand and one) in which you first felt unloved or unlovable. It is from these experiences that the mind develops the illusion of an inadequate supply of love.

A drowning person experiences an inadequate supply of air. A hungry person experiences an inadequate supply of food. While we may not have experienced starvation or drowning, nearly all of us have hungered for love and drowned for lack of recognition. Humanity in general seems to be most stingy on the issue of giving .and receiving love, so that it is possible to grow up in economic affluence while experiencing a permanent poverty in regard to love and recognition.

We experience situations where love is in short supply. The mind decides that there is not enough to go around. Then we base our future actions on that decision. We also make up reasons to make that decision more sensible. We think,

Maybe I really am unlovable.
Well, anybody who did that must surely be unlovable.
If everybody thinks I'm that way, maybe I must really be that way.

Reasons are positions the mind takes when under stress. Whenever it is confused or in too much pain to look at what is really going on, the mind will make up a reason to make things fit a little better. Reasons are a retreat to a safe position. It is an illusory safety, though, because reasons are not true and real. Ultimately, in order to grow, we have to go beyond all our reasons.

In learning to love yourself you will always be running up against the next biggest reason why you should not love yourself, just as in relationship to another person you will always be coming up against the next barrier to loving them. Learning to love always feels a little risky, even outlandish at times. We think, I could never love myself for *that,* or, I could never accept *that* about another person.

You will always be having the opportunity to go beyond the illusory safety of reasons into the real safety of love. You will always be discovering the next wall of reasons, then vaulting over into a new place: loving yourself anyway.

Be careful not to use reasons to tell yourself why you're lovable. It is never satisfying, because you are using reason to fight reason. (Example: "Even though I hate myself, my friends seem to like me, so that must mean I'm lovable.") The alternative is to go right past reason and love yourself for being the way you are. Simply love yourself, regardless of reason. Love yourself for hating yourself, for not being able to love yourself. Love yourself for all the crazy reasons you don't love yourself. Reasons are a retreat to an imaginary safety, when all the time the real safety of love is there if we are willing to expand into it. No matter what tricks your mind tries in order to keep you from realizing this fact, you can experience the truth of it any time, any place, in any mood, by simply opening up in love to yourself at that moment.

CHAPTER SEVEN
Learning To Love Yourself 'Live'

There Is nothing quite like the moment when someone has the experience of loving himself or herself. I have seen this hundreds of times in therapy and workshops, and it continues to be one of the most moving things In my life. I thought that you, the reader, might like to drop in on some of these moments. What follows are tape-recorded from therapy sessions or workshops. The people involved, whose names are changed, kindly gave permission for their transcript to be used.

The first transcript is from a workshop which I offer now and then called "The Experience of Loving Yourself." The characters: an engineer named Jack, facing a roomful of workshop participants, and me in the back of the room. During this phase of the workshop, I work with each person Individually, and Jack has volunteered. He first asks me to clarify our purpose:

GAY: Our purpose during this part of the workshop is to clear up any barriers in the way of your loving yourself right now and to give you the opportunity to experience loving yourself.

JACK: Okay. First, I do want to learn to love myself. Fact Is, I've wanted that for a long time. In my own mind, I don't have to elaborate or prove

GAY: Hold on a second. I liked the clarity of your first statement. Then I heard you move off into an elaboration and explanation of that. I think the first statement was very powerful and stands on its own and needs no elaboration. What I would recommend is that you make that statement again and wait for the experience. Without any words, without any elaboration, without any mind-stuff. Would you be willing to try that?

JACK: Yes.

GAY: Good. Let's hear it.

JACK: I do want to experience loving myself right now.

GAY: Good. (To other participants) In order to assist Jack in this, as if to blow on the coals and get the flame going, I'd like us all to focus our intense love on him. Open your hearts to him, loving him the way he is. You know some about who he is, what he does, who he isn't, and I'd like you to forget all that and just love him. (Several of the participants go up and hug him.)

GAY: See what happens when you put out what you want straight and clear? You don't have to do it all alone. I think that some of the experiences you've had would lead you to believe it has to be a solo venture.

(Long pause while Jack stands with his eyes closed. He appears to be assimilating the impact of the experience he has just had.)

GAY: Do you feel loving toward yourself right now?

JACK: I feel surprised that you could come up and love me like that. That each of you would express love to me.

GAY: Do you love yourself right now for feeling that surprise? (Long pause)

JACK: I'm having difficulty with that.

GAY: Could you love yourself for having difficulty with that? (Long pause)

JACK: I feel accepted, and I feel afraid of that acceptance.

GAY: Would you be willing to love yourself for feeling accepted and afraid of that acceptance?

(Long pause. The tension in the room has everyone's eyes riveted on Jack. It is becoming clear to everyone that one of Jack's main issues in life, his tendency to intellectualize and turn away people's love, is being acted out in front of them.)

JACK: I'm afraid to love.

GAY: Can you love yourself for that?

JACK: I'm telling myself I don't know how.

GAY: Can you love yourself for that right now?

JACK: What is love?

GAY: Would you be willing to love yourself for not knowing what love is?

(Long pause)

JACK: I have a message in me that says "You have to work it out for yourself."

GAY: Can you love yourself for having that message? Would you be willing to love yourself right now for having that experience? (Long pause)

GAY: Notice, Jack, that in each of the questions I've asked you, the appropriate answer is yes or no. And in each one of them you redefined my question and elaborated when no elaboration was called for. That's the tendency of the big brain to want to escape the inevitable, which is the experience of loving yourself. Best now to put your big brain on hold and open yourself to the experience. The big brain no longer works in this situation.

Your big brain has in fact failed miserably in helping you learn to love yourself.

JACK: Part of the reason I grind away at it is that I don't have very much confidence in my mind.

GAY: Good. Would you be willing to love yourself right now for not having any confidence in your mind?

JACK: No.

GAY: Would you be willing to love yourself for not being able to love yourself?

JACK: No.

GAY: Would you be willing to love yourself for not being willing to love yourself?

JACK: No. I'm puzzled.

GAY: Good. Would you be willing to love yourself for the experience of being puzzled?
(Long pause)

JACK: Yes. (He and the participants break into smiles.)

GAY: Take a couple of deep breaths of love for yourself. Taste the feeling of love for yourself being puzzled. (Pause)

GAY: What do you feel in your body when you feel love for yourself?

JACK: Space. An opening.

GAY: Good. Thank you.

(Jack sits down to ringing applause.)

Comments: This work was something of a breakthrough for Jack. It gave him a moment's taste of the experience of puzzlement and wonder, which he had always rushed to bury beneath a bushel of intellectualizations and explanations. He was able to get beyond his mind for a moment and say "I don't know."

Jack had several immediate results in his life from this moment. He had been obsessed for fifteen years with an unsolvable problem. He broke the obsession with this one moment of loving himself for feeling puzzled. His relationship with his wife also improved significantly after the workshop.

The next transcript is from a session with an attractive woman in her twenties. Member of a glamorous profession, she has some deep-seated fears she would like to be rid of.

GAY: What would you like to work on?

CLAUDIA: I would like to learn to love myself for doing nothing. All my life I feel like I've been rewarded for doing tricks for people.

GAY: So you were one of those people who got a lot of strokes when you were growing up for dressing right, doing it right....

CLAUDIA: Yes, I got my love by looking cute, being funny, saying the right thing, being real supportive of my mother.

GAY: How does all that affect your life today?

CLAUDIA: Sometimes I lie. Like, I'll be angry with somebody and instead of telling them_ I'm angry, I'll be real supportive with them because I'm afraid I'll lose their love. I feel like I'm filled with fear all the time. If I feel like I'm going to get close to people, I feel afraid. I've done that now with the women's group I'm in. There reaches a point in the relationship where I've felt their love, then I get scared I'm going to lose it. I'm afraid to almost move.... I'm afraid I'll say the wrong thing.... I'm that way with my women's group-I go in there every week and I feel panic-stricken. Sharing myself, anything that's going on with me, is really hard.

GAY: It sounds like you are leading up to a resolution of some sort of major issue in your life. It's coming up stronger and stronger, seeking resolution.

CLAUDIA: I think it's already happening. Yesterday It came to a head when I had a situation where I just couldn't control myself. (Claudia begins to cry.) I just couldn't *seem* to get love from somebody I wanted it from. I think I just came to the realization that I've got to stop controlling other people. I can't get love that way anyway.

I'm having to let go and just go Into space, and it's a fearful place to be. I keep grabbing on to people and things for security. Like today, I'm trying not to be In that space-I'm trying to be good because I'm here-but it's not working.

GAY: It's mostly a fear place-you feel really scared.

CLAUDIA: Mmm-hmm.

GAY: So all of that trying to be cute and so forth, it all comes out of that experience of fear.

CLAUDIA: Yes.

GAY: Right now, Claudia, if the floor were shaking, you'd reach out for support. You'd grab on to some structure.

CLAUDIA: Mmm-hmm.

GAY: And after a while, if the floor were still shaking and you decided you'd had enough structure and you wanted to test out your ability to stand on a shaky floor-just for the adventure of it-well, that process of letting go of structure involves a burst of fear.

When you let go of control, you get a rush of fear. Previously you believed that if you maintained control, the fear would be less. Actually that's not true. The truth seems to be that the control doesn't keep the fear down, it just numbs you. You don't feel the fear as much because you're numb. In fact, the only way to deal with the fear is let go of the control, ride out that burst of fear, then shake with the floor as long as it's shaking. Then you're through it, because the floor doesn't usually shake very long.

CLAUDIA: I feel like I've pretty much completed the earthquake, but I'm scared I'm going to go back to that real scared feeling. Yesterday I went into that state for an hour or two. I was real sad and everything, I felt hopeless.

GAY: Try an experiment, if you will. I'd like you to stand with your feet planted sturdily. If you were feeling an earthquake, you wouldn't stand with your feet so close together.

Instead of trying to make the fear go away, open up to it, say hello to it.

CLAUDIA: I'm not sure I can do that. My fear is it *won't* go away.

GAY: Yes, I know. That belief has been around for a long time. But now let's just open up to that fear, invite it, explore it. No effort required, just shining a little light on it.

CLAUDIA: I have a pain in my back.

GAY: Yes, probably resistance to the fear.

CLAUDIA: I don't like it.

GAY: Good. See if you can love yourself for those two things.

Love yourself for not liking it, and for the fear, too.

CLAUDIA: I don't understand. Can you explain?

GAY: Yes. You feel scared, and then on top of that you don't like feeling scared, and then on top of that you don't like working on that feeling.

See how you do with loving yourself for feeling scared. Say "I love myself for feeling scared."

CLAUDIA: I love myself for feeling scared.

GAY: Try that again.

CLAUDIA: I love myself for feeling scared.

GAY: Yes. You know, Claudia, I get a whole different sense of your way of being when you say that. You even stand different. Before you looked like daddy's little girl instead of Claudia. When you take responsibility for your fear, feel it and love it, you take charge of yourself.

CLAUDIA: It feels different. I feel powerful now.

GAY: Yes, and it requires nothing from others. You don't need to be helped out of your fear. You don't have to manipulate. CLAUDIA: What feels good is that I can say I'm scared without having to say why or understand it.

GAY: Yes, anybody who thinks they know all the reasons they're scared is nuts. You can have those feelings and don't need to explain them.

The thing to remember is: Go beyond reasons to love. The way you are is perfect. A good way to know if you're growing or not is if you're scared. Not being scared isn't an option on this planet. There are only two kinds of people—those that are scared and admit it and open up to it, and those that are scared and shut down to it.

The next tape is from a woman of about thirty who is a commercial artist. The problem she presents involves her difficulties with a relationship she's in with a man.

ALICE: The thing I want to work on has to do with loving myself, I think. I'm in a relationship, and I can't seem to get out of it, nor can I seem to let it be good. Also, I have the feeling all the time that people don't like me. I know a lot of the time that's not true, but I'm always ready to think so.

GAY: Mmm-hmm. As I listened to you talk, Alice, my attention was drawn to your face. It has right now what I would call a masklike quality. I'm wondering if there was some time back in your life when you decided to go behind a mask. My sense is that you have a lot of life, a lot of buzz inside you, and you keep it hidden behind your face and those big glasses. Are you aware of holding your face stiff and masklike?

ALICE: Not really. Once in a while I notice it. I can feel it now, though.

GAY: I can see a battle going on between the energy underneath the mask and the tension to keep that energy under control. Are you aware of what was going on when you decided to put up the mask?

ALICE: I think it was a thing between me and my mother. I was always reaching out to her, and I think she had a lot of problems with letting herself love me. So I always felt like I had to hold back.

GAY: Yes. Alice, what's going on In your body right now?

ALICE: My legs are trembling. I feel a lot of vibrations starting to move up and down my body.

GAY: It seems like one of your major fears is that if you open up to relationships outside of you, you will lose contact with who you are inside. You made that decision a long time ago. It no longer serves you now. I'd like you to know that you can open up to giving and getting love from others, and it doesn't need to take you out of your relationship with yourself. In other words, you don't have to hide inside anymore.

           How are you feeling right now?

ALICE: I feel tingling all over my body.

GAY: Yes. Here's the point where you can go beyond reason to love, although it doesn't make sense. I'd like you to love yourself for how you're feeling right now.

(Long pause. Finally Alice laughs delightedly.)

GAY: Try an experiment, if you will. Pick a person at random and tell them you love them.

ALICE: (Looks at a workshop participant) I love you. (She laughs again.)

GAY: What do you feel?

ALICE: I can love somebody else and myself, at the same time.

GAY: Yes. Do you feel any fear?

ALICE: No.

GAY: Yes. Let's remember that. At the moment of expressing love, to yourself or someone else, there is no fear. Love cancels out fear.

           Thank you, Alice.

ALICE: Thank you.

A moment of loving oneself, though it may be over before you know it, has long-term, life-changing consequences. Here is an eloquent description of such a moment and its aftermath, written by a gifted therapist of my acquaintance named Katy.

I feel a tangible joy about loving myself. It seems to have dissolved or taken the space of fear and worry. I have a sensory experience of cycles of electrical energy rising up the center of my body, as well as many other physical manifestations: shifts in the proportions of my body, changes in the color of my skin, and a steady increase in my general energy level. At the same time my mind operates both very quickly and very slowly, taking shortcuts through superficial data and yet also focusing panoramically on the detail. All this seems held within a space which is empty of thought except for occasional phrases that arise like blessings: "I'm enough," "It doesn't matter," "It's all love." The empty space seems to be *love,* the vibration of active waiting, resting potential, the source.

Love is opening my heart, my throat, and other body centers. I find myself more expressibly loving, more interested in just what is happening in each moment, becoming one with people more often in the daily routines of supermarket and traffic.

I feel more space under and around my experience. I go through cycles of expanding to embrace more of life, then contracting to keep my individual identity, expanding again, contracting. My life now feels like an unfolding of opportunities to become more unified with what is, more whole, while at the same time learning to express and give the overflow out into the universe.

I had directed all my love toward others as a way of getting them to approve of me. I didn't know how to direct that approval and tenderness toward myself. My conditioning had taught me that *real* love meant duty, obedience, submission, sacrificing for the sake of others, giving my spark to others without getting anything in return. I gave the power to validate me to others with whom I was in relationship. I focused on the person whose approval I sought; he made the world go around for me. I shut down my full breathing capacity, trading in my own vitality for the pseudo-vitality of riding on someone else's power. The hopeful, compelling sweetness of the victim position put me in a trance that I chose instead of the uncertainty of the actual feeling of aliveness.

What *led up* to my experience of learning to love myself was a therapy session in which I had the inescapable realization that no one else is going to do it for me in life; I am the source. My experience now is of extending that unconditional love toward myself and allowing its effects, allowing myself to feel complete and belonging in the world. I welcome myself as able, strong *and soft,* steely, pure.

A recent experience of loving myself under stress involved a tug of feelings about my mate's seeing another woman. My internal dialogue went like this: Why is he choosing her over me? He must not really love me, or he would be here. If he really loved me, he *would* not be interested in anybody else. Another voice is saying Notice, notice where you are right now. I am also literally rocking myself back and forth, holding and supporting my experience, allowing my feelings to be, to have their voice. First voice again: He must not approve of who I am—wham, breakthrough, flash of knowing—I see that this is about early issues of being abandoned, not wanted. Okay. I direct my awareness to that old place, that need, and love that part of me as fully as I can. I acknowledge it, attend to it, not interfering. I recall a conversation: "Pain and love are two sides of a polarity. Once you are willing to experience both completely, a space opens which holds both love and pain." I say yes to it all. As I breathe and love myself, the feeling of jealousy transmutes, and I feel bliss.

CHAPTER EIGHT
Learning To Love Yourself
While Being In Love

Intimate relationships have been for me the greatest challenge in learning and remembering to love myself. I have come across the most unlovable parts of myself while relating with the people who have been closest to me. Too, it seems that as soon as I reach a new level of learning to love myself, I invite into my life the very person who can push my "unlovable" button at a deeper level. For a long time I puzzled over that fact. Now I see that it makes exquisite sense. Here's why.

We come into intimate relationships to satisfy certain basic desires. We seek an intense experience of self: to have others see us as who we really are and to see others as who they really are. We want to go beyond the masks of the personality and be accepted at our essence. But when this actually starts to happen, we tend to slam on the brakes. Why? Because we fear most deeply that which most deeply attracts us. So we are attracted to that deep experience of self, and, simultaneously, we repel it.

The only way to find our way down through the masks to find the real self within is by placing ourselves in a situation where we get to see the masks. We do this in many ways, such as meditation, therapy, workshops, and reading. One powerful way to illuminate our masks is to enter an intimate relationship. For when you get close to someone, no matter whether a lover, a family member, or a friend, you bring up into awareness the very barriers that must be dissolved in order to relate to that person's true self with your own true self. In other words, as you get closer, 'you will always bring up the next biggest thing you need to learn to love about yourself. Whether this fact delights or maddens you is up to you. I have experienced both reactions myself, but it still did nothing to change the fact.

The barrier on which I will focus is the one with which I am most familiar, both in my own life and in the lives of people with whom I have worked. It is the projection barrier; I have seen relationships completely destroyed because of it, and others completely transformed by getting through it.

Let's say that you are afraid of rejection. This is a deep fear that goes far back in your life. Never mind where it came from-mother, father, first-grade teacher. Something happens to cause you to fear rejection. There is a creative part of your mind, way down in the unconscious, that is always seeking opportunities to work out these kinds of old issues. It will lead you into situations where you have the opportunity to bring that fear into your awareness. It will likely lead you into a situation where rejection is a possibility or, if not, where you can make it a possibility. Clearly this is creative; clearly this is good. Clearly we hate it.

When we get into the situation-which we have created ourselves-we put on the brakes and begin to wail that we have been "unfaired against," in the memorable words of one of my clients. We thereby take an opportunity for growth that we have ingeniously devised for ourselves and turn it into a mistake by thinking that it is a mistake.

Worse yet, we will usually blame it on the other person. This is where projection comes in. Whenever there is something we cannot accept about ourselves, we will tend to project it on someone outside ourselves. So if we cannot accept our sexuality, we will see others as depraved. If our own anger is too much for us to accept, we will see a lot of angry people out there in the world. Projection is the rule rather than the exception in the world. There is frighteningly little genuine responsibility taken by us in our relationships with others. We can certainly see this in the realm of politics, where nations blame other nations for their own outrageous crimes. But we can see it closer to home by observing how we go about our relationships with our own close ones.

Ideally, when trouble arises in a relationship, we should begin to ask questions of ourselves:

What is it here that I am not willing to accept in myself?
What am I having the opportunity to learn to love about myself?
What part of myself am I projecting onto the other person? What am I seeing that I am unwilling to admit is part of me?

Instead, though, we often begin to perceive ourselves as the victim. As soon as we occupy the victim position, our partner has little choice but to make a run for that position too. Arguments are usually based on the issue of who gets to be the victim.

Unfortunately, we often resolve disputes by deciding that one person actually has been victimized by the other. While this may work just fine in cases of burglary, rape, and other crimes, it works very poorly in most of our personal problems. In personal issues our greatest learning will occur when both parties are able to abandon the illusory safety of the victim position and take genuine responsibility for their role in the problem. Even in a case where there is a seemingly clear-cut victim, if we look a little closer we may learn something profound.

I am thinking as an example of a man whose wife had an affair with another man. He had never had a relationship with another woman other than his wife, so we may inquire, as he did, as to how he was in any way responsible for that situation. He began by perceiving himself as the victim, and although that position felt good for a while, it was not very satisfying in the long run. He began to suspect that there were other things in the situation that needed to be looked at. What he saw was a revelation to him, and he changed not only his relationship with his wife but the rest of his life as well.

When he inquired deeply into it, he saw that he had always had an unconscious and certainly unspoken belief that his wife would someday cheat on him. He saw the origin of that belief in a remarkably similar situation between his mother and father. His mother had had an affair while his father was off in a war. The son (my client) had known about it, and only later had the father found out about it. The son had witnessed a bitter battle between the parents and had completely forgotten about it until the situation with his wife thirty years later.

In a dance neither person is "causing" the other person to dance; In this situation neither party caused the other to do what he or she did. They just danced together for a period of time to work out various issues they needed to work out. There is no need, then, when watching a dance, to figure out who is dancing whom. The victim dance is even more difficult to figure out. It is never possible to figure out who is the bigger victim. The only solution is for each party to take one-hundred percent responsibility.

Relationships work when each person is willing to see that each is an equal creator of all aspects of the relationship. Relationships don't work when anybody takes less than one-hundred-percent responsibility. Learning to love yourself in a relationship is seeing that you will create the very situations you need that allow you to experience the parts of yourself you cannot love. By doing that you will eventually have the opportunity to love all of yourself. Then, as if by magic, you will find yourself being completely loved by others.

CHAPTER NINE
A Short Psychology Of Forgiveness

Forgiveness is one of the most beautiful experiences open to us as humans. It cleanses, heals, and strengthens bonds. We typically find forgiveness difficult to practice, though. No matter how many times we hear about its virtues, no matter how often we see its beneficial results, we still have other people and things in ourselves-which we cannot forgive. What prevents us from putting forgiveness into practice more often?

It looks to me that our main problem is that we get stuck in trying to forgive before we accept our own feelings exactly as they are. Thinking that we should forgive, attempting forgiveness, prevents us from having the actual experience of it. If I am angry and hurt after an interaction with my wife, I must first deal with my own feelings in the situation before I can have the experience of forgiving her. I must open up to accept my anger and hurt; I must get to the bottom of my own experience. I may need to communicate about my experience with her. Then, coming from a place of clarity, I can come naturally to a state of forgiveness. That is, by taking care of my own experience in a loving way, I can slip into the experience of forgiveness spontaneously and organically.

I have seen this happen many times in my own life and in the lives of people I see in counseling. Recently I was feeling stuck in my relationship with my wife. Try as I might, I could not seem to forgive her or generate any good will toward her. So after wrestling with it for a while, I saw that I was trying hard to be some way I wasn't. I decided to take things as they were. Quickly feelings began to emerge. I felt anger, then more anger, then I felt a layer of deep hurt. As I let myself experience these feelings, I began to feel lighter in my body and mind. A sense of satisfaction came over me. Then for a day or two I did not think about the situation much at all. Suddenly one morning I realized that I felt good will toward her again. I felt again that warmth and well-wishing toward her that I like to feel. I think I came naturally to that space by giving up the effort to forgive and being willing to deal with whatever was there.

Surely this lesson must be one of the most difficult we have to learn. It seems that our whole lives have been spent learning how to deny or ignore our own experience in order to impose some ideal state upon it. There is nothing particularly sacred about our own experience, but if we deny or ignore it, we will have to come back later and deal with it in some way. If we forgive someone or turn the other cheek at our own expense, we will not feel satisfied, and we will miss out on the beauty of the experience of true forgiveness.

Spontaneous, organic forgiveness takes place free of effort. It flows naturally when we achieve completeness with feelings with which we were previously incomplete. In short, forgiveness flows from being willing to know the truth and tell the truth.

CHAPTER TEN
The Experience Of Oneness

There is a bonus for learning to love ourselves, for the act of welcoming into ourselves all the unloved parts of us. It is the experience of oneness; it is the finest thing of which I personally know.

We cannot predict when or if the feeling of oneness may come upon us. I know that for me it was preceded by hundreds of little experiences of befriending and loving different previously disowned parts of myself. Then suddenly one day it was upon me without warning, a sweet and powerful sensation that rolled over me like a wave, changing everything in its path.

As I wrote at the time:

Having *felt* oneness does
   not mean you will *never* again
      argue with your spouse,
      stub your toe,
      or have your hubcap stolen.
But you will know that now and then the one
      argues with *itself*,
      stubs its toe,
      steals hubcaps from itself.
There is no more us versus them,
    no more in and out.
      All is healed.
      All is one.

Or, as I wrote on another day after my first experience of oneness:

Once you know you're one,
   All is changed
         and still the same.

Now it appears to me that oneness is chasing us. If we run from it, that's all right (the one runs from itself). Sometime, though, you will want to slow down and let it overtake you. Wholeness is chasing us. The disowned wolves of our dark inner forests are baying for recognition. Bow to them and watch their ferocity dissolve. If we face them with a smile, we can see that they are really part of us. We can learn from them.

When we try to outrun ourselves, we get tired. When we get tired, we may hurt each other and ourselves. But if we look closely, we can see that all these things that are pursuing us are really parts of ourselves, especially those things that seem most outside of us.

As I travel through the world I see many things I want to disown: poverty, pain, cruelty, hunger. All I can do is greet my revulsion with love and welcome it into the oneness of me. When I do that, I see that all poverty, pain, cruelty, and hunger exist within me. Then perhaps I can help, because I can see those I wish to help as equals. As the poet Rumi said seven hundred years ago, "My small heart is part of the larger." I would add, "To expand my small heart is to expand the larger."

To open ourselves is to invite a feeling of unity to come upon us. When we have rejoiced in that wholeness, our next impulse is to reach out and include others in our oneness. Perhaps one day all humanity will be united in one big dance of oneness-ourselves, each other, and the universe itself. Until then, all we can do, all we need to do, is to continue opening in love to ourselves and our neighbors.

CHAPTER ELEVEN
Seeing Death Clearly

A poor relationship with death eliminates the possibility of a clear and passionate relationship with life. Unless we see death clearly, we are destined to see life through a fog as well. We must ask ourselves what obscures our view of death, so that we may cut through the fog and deal with what is real.

Some of the fog around death is due to our thoughts, some to our feelings. Let us look at thoughts first, because they occur at a more superficial level than feelings. Once we have illuminated the shadows cast by thoughts, we can explore the deeper obscurities of our feelings.

Much thought comes from incomplete experiences. When we leave behind experiences we have not completed, we create a breeding ground for thoughts. For example, if I have an argument with my wife and do not tell her everything that I am upset about, I will replay the argument later in my mind, perhaps a hundred times. Each time I will edit the tape a little to prove a point or to ensure my victory. We could say that my leaving some things unsaid generated subsequent thoughts. Had I communicated everything I had to say at the time, I would not have needed to carry on the argument later in my head.

Death, because of its infinite nature, is perhaps the most difficult thing in life with which to reach any sort of completion. I invite you to try an experiment with me. I will now settle back in my chair and think about death, attempting to see it clearly and steadily. Perhaps you could do that, too, so that we may jointly experience some of the difficulties we face. (Threeminute pause.)

First, I could not get my mind to consider death. So I said the word "death" to myself. Immediately my mind jumped to a thought of my friends Peter and Gina and their new baby. I thought of how much I wanted to see them, how I'd wanted to call them but had forgotten. Then my mind came back to death, and a shudder of anxiety swept up through my chest. My mind was off again then, playing some music, first a rock tune, then a snatch from a Bach concert I attended last night. "Death," I said again, engendering another gust of anxiety. Pictures of my grandmother's death floated through my mind.

So it goes. This quick experience shows us something of the elusive quality of seeing death clearly. The mind does not want to see clearly its own demise. Perhaps it cannot. Perhaps it is futile to try to get a clear sense of anything so infinitely mysterious as death. I would like to go as far as I can, though, because I sense a much deeper connection with life awaiting me if I can only come to completion with death.

Some of our thoughts about death come from memories of the experiences we have had with it. A relative's funeral, an accident, the stories we have heard about deaths in our family-all these experiences provide the fuel for memories in the mind.

Other thoughts about death come from the beliefs we have adapted over the years as we listened to the teachings of family and church. On this side of the world the primary religions' teaching about death is that it is a separation of body and soul. Body is left behind; soul goes forth to a happy or painful fate in another world. On the other side of the world the dominant belief about death is that it is another milestone in a series of incarnations. The soul in its evolution goes through stage after stage, taking on a body for a certain set of lessons, then dropping the body and incarnating in a fresh one for a new set of learnings.

In either case, whether in the Western idea of heaven and hell or in the Eastern idea of reincarnation, the issues are the same. There is something in us that does not end when the body stops working. Some part of us continues to *experience,* either coming back for another life in a body, as in reincarnation, or entering a heavenly or hellish eternity, as in the Western tradition.

But let us look at this more closely. What is actually going on here? First, we have a fact that we can agree upon: bodies stop working. They decay, and in civilized societies they are generally burned or buried. The agreement stops here. Next comes the part where the speculation begins. Some say reincarnation is the process, others say heaven or hell. Many others refuse to play the speculation game at all. The body is a machine, they say, and eventually the machine stops working. That's it.

How do we get from the fact of death that we can agree on to the fantasies about death that we argue about? If we can find this out, we will be able to see death more clearly.

I believe that I can see how it works, at least in myself. Try it on and see if it fits for you. When we are faced with the fact of death, when we see that the body and the brain (our body! our brain!) stop working, we feel scared. When I think of my mind ceasing to hum, the same mind which fell in love and tasted Dom Perignon and listened to Bach and knew my grandmother's love, I feel terribly afraid. What is the point of it all? So it appears that our mind, the main job of which is to experience, flips on the fear switch when it thinks about not experiencing. I am afraid of not experiencing, of not even being able to experience nothing, and I am afraid that I will be left out, that life will go on without me. I do not like to be left out.

In the face of the facts of death we feel fear. Any time there is a feeling, there are also wants and needs. What is it that we find ourselves wanting in the face of this fear? I think we want experience. I think we have had in our lives so little taste of what it means to really experience life that the idea of dying terrifies us. So our minds make up a story to ease us. Experience, even hellish experience, is easier for the mind to handle than no experience at all.

Here is what we have so far:

Fact of death -+ fear -' mind makes up a story to ease itself

The two major stories the mind has made up so far are reincarnation and heaven/hell.

Just a moment. Does this mean that there is no reality to either of these stories? Are we saying that these stories are just a pack of lies to get the body out of its fear? Yes and no. Either of these stories could be true, or there could be an infinity of true stories. But we can only get to the truth by being willing to conceive that what we believe is a lie. Otherwise we are simply stuck in our beliefs. We must want to fit a picture of the way our minds work that is so close to being the way they actually work that it allows us to jump beyond the current way it works into something new. So far we have the fact of death, our fears of death, our craving for experience, and the stories the mind makes up to assuage the body. On top of all this, what could give rise to the notion that existence is continuous, that there could be something within but also beyond the body that keeps on experiencing? To find the answer to this question we must go down deep into our consciousness.

I close my eyes and relax into myself for a moment. I say in my mind, I'm scared of dying. A wave of fear rolls up through my body and breaks in my mind. Suddenly my mind is a jumble of thoughts: things I must do today, music, decisions, worries. I see that those thoughts are an escape from opening up more deeply to the fear of dying. So I reel my mind in and settle back into the feeling of fear. Another wave, stronger this time. And another. Now my body is alive with wave after wave of sensation. I open up and love myself for feeling scared of dying. The waves turn into bliss, then peace. Now I am full of a clear, light sensation. No thoughts, just pure being.

So underneath all the stories in the mind about death, at the bottom of the fear, there is a clear space, a place where we simply are. Could this clear space be the source of our ideas about the existence of a soul separate from the body? Perhaps. There is something about that clear space that feels permanent, as if it is synonymous with the space that pervades the universe.

Now I believe I am beginning to see it. When we are living in our beliefs, before we are willing to see the fact of death, we make it an either-or thing. Either we die (the body stops working) or we live on. Now I see that, as we cut down through beliefs, open up to the fear, and get to the bottom of it, there is a possibility that both are true. Beyond that I cannot see.

I know this, though. At the bottom of all my fantasies and feelings about death there was that clear space; and I have been there before. It is the source of joy, creativity, and passion.

It feels to me to be where life itself comes from, so I can see why we think it is where life goes.

How does all of this help us with life? In every conceivable way. The very process of seeing death clearly is the process of seeing life clearly. In order to live with passion, we must get beyond our beliefs about life and go deeply into the experience of it. At the bottom of our experience of all of life, the beauty and the pain, there is the source of all life. When we are willing to be the source of life, we can become a fountain of creativity ourselves and also an inspiration to people around us.

In addition, by acknowledging the facts of death we see that we crave experience. In the face of no experience we will make up stories about it so that we will not have to face the possibility of no experience. The magnificent surprise at the heart of the matter is this: we can give ourselves the gift of experience right now in life. One reason no experience sounds so awful to us is that we are afraid to experience deeply right now in life. By facing this fear and going through it to the other side, we see that we can give ourselves permission to experience life so deeply that perhaps in time we may come to have such a clear and passionate relationship with life that death itself can be viewed with the same clarity and passion.

CHAPTER TWELVE
Experiments In Loving Yourself

Reading about learning to love yourself can lay the essential groundwork for the actual experience of it. I hope by now your reading has triggered many experiences of loving various aspects of yourself. If you would enjoy experimenting further, I would like to share with you some of the activities that I have found useful in classes and workshops. These experiments have been considered the most fun and the most helpful by participants in various classes. Some are to be done in the quiet of your own mind, while others need the participation of a partner.

Remember: A good experiment is one in which you learn something, no matter what the results are.

EXPERIMENT ONE

A Love Meditation

Begin by sitting quietly in a place where you will not be likely to be disturbed for ten minutes or so. Close your eyes and give your mind a minute to settle down. Then say the following sentence in your mind every ten to fifteen seconds.

I love myself

After each repetition of that sentence, rest quietly for ten to fifteen seconds and experience what happens in your mind and body. Does your mind say "no, I don't"? Does your leg start to itch? Do you feel a rush of joy? There are no right answers here, no experience you are supposed to have. All you are doing is seeing what happens when you take the position that you love yourself.

Try the experiment for a few minutes, then gently return your awareness to the outside. Think over the results or share them. with a friend.

EXPERIMENT TWO

A Second Love Meditation

Begin by sitting quietly with your eyes closed. Let your mind settle down for a minute or so, then say the following incomplete sentence in your mind every ten seconds.

I love myself for...

After each repetition, pause to see how your mind fills in the blank. After it does (or doesn't), simply repeat the sentence again.

Here are a few ways my mind filled in the sentences when I recently tried the experiment.

I love myself for loving myself.
I love myself for hating myself.
I love myself for feeling sleepy.
I love myself for being hungry.
I love myself for feeling good.

You might think of this experiment as a way of clearing space inside and finding out all the ways you love yourself. After you have done it for a few minutes, let your awareness return to the outside again.

EXPERIMENT THREE

Love In Writing

This experiment uses the medium of writing to help us experience self-love. Take a paper and pencil and complete the following sentence about ten times. Let your mind go wild and see how many different ways you can fill in the blank.

I would love myself if
(Examples: I would love myself if I weren't an alcoholic.
I would love myself if I weren't so fat.)

After you have done that, go back and write the following sentence, filling the blank with the same things you wrote above.

I love myself for _____

In other words, if you wrote "I would love myself if I weren't so fat" in the first part of the experiment, switch it to "I love myself for being so fat" in the second part. No matter how difficult it seems, try to write each one.

EXPERIMENT FOUR

Love In Action

Stand or sit facing a partner. Make eye contact and say the following sentence about ten or fifteen times. Pause five or ten seconds between each repetition.

I love myself...

Have your partner give you feedback at the end about what he or she noticed about you after each repetition. Did your eyes blink? Did you lose eye contact?

Switch and give your partner a chance to try it.
Afterwards discuss your findings. You might also try some other sentences, such as
I love myself deeply.
I love myself no matter how I act.
I am completely lovable.
I am willing to give and receive love fully.

EXPERIMENT FIVE
Drawing Love

You will need a big piece of paper and some crayons for this activity. Begin by drawing a big, preferably life-size picture of your body. Then pick a color that represents love and one that represents unlove. Using the two colors, color in the lovable and unlovable parts of your body. In other words, if you are using green for love and grey for unlove, you might color your legs green if you love them, while coloring your chest grey if you do not love that part of you.

EXPERIMENT SIX
Cataloging Your Love

Make two columns on a piece of paper. Title the first column "Unlovable Things about Me" and title the second column "Lovable Things about Me." For example:

Unlovable Things about Me	Lovable Things about Me
My greediness	The way I care for my dog
My legs	My hair
The way I dance	My ability to solve problems
My sarcasm	

The purpose of this experiment is to help you identify the parts of you that need love.

CHAPTER THIRTEEN
Questions And Answers

Isn't it conceited to love yourself?

Being conceited is attempting to prove to the world that you are okay after you have come to feel that you are unlovable. There is a fundamental gap between how you feel inside and what you are presenting to the outside world. As you feel more genuine love for yourself you have less need to prove your lovableness to the outside world. It shows naturally.

*Is learning to love yourself the same thing
as "positive thinking"?*

Some approaches to "positive thinking" would have us ignore the negative thought or replace it with a positive one: if we think, I don't like Jack, we would ignore it or think something positive about Jack instead. In learning to love ourselves we take what is there and love our way through it, rather than ignoring it or rushing to replace it with something more pleasant. So we might love ourselves first for the dislike we feel. This act gives space to our reaction rather than crowding it out. Loving it the way it is allows us to learn from it.

What do I do when I am hating myself?

One thing you can do is love yourself for hating yourself. Hate is part of life, too. Love can contain it. Nothing that can be experienced is too big for love to contain. It holds everything.

What can I do when I can't remember how to love myself?

The quick ticket to ecstasy is to catch yourself feeling in a very low state of mind-depressed, stupid, hateful-and to love yourself for feeling just that way. When you do that you can experience a rocket ride right to the top. Love does not take time; it's possible to transform depression into ecstasy in a flash. But please do not accept my word for it. Try it as an experiment next time you are feeling low.

Something else to consider is that we will always be in the process of remembering how to love ourselves, then forgetting, then remembering again. It does not seem to be our destiny to be any one way all the time. So let's get used to being pendulums and enjoy the ride.

How do you learn to love a person you hate?

A key question. The idea of "Love your neighbor" is noble but difficult. It has engendered a great deal of guilt in well-meaning people who find themselves unable to put the proverb into practice. The reason it does not usually work is that it asks us to skip over our own feelings and adopt a positive attitude toward the neighbor without regard to our own position.

The way out of this is to love ourselves first for our reactions. Then perhaps we can love our neighbor. When we try to love our neighbor before loving ourselves, we are coming from a very weak base. If I am angry at my neighbor, or scared of him, I will not be able to love him until I have come to terms with my own feelings. Loving your neighbor is the ideal; loving yourself first is the way to put it into practice.

How do I get rid of feelings. I don't want to have?

Let's look carefully at the notion of getting rid of feelings. It seems that what we want in this situation is to stop experiencing something we find troublesome. Paradoxically, the only way to stop experiencing something is to be totally willing to experience it.

In fact, we will never be rid of anything. Even if we do not feel fear, for example, for twenty years, the potential for feeling it will still be there. So there is no way, we can be totally rid of anything. On the other hand, there is no reason to be rid of anything. What we really want is to be expanded enough so that all our feelings can take place within us without troubling us. That is what becoming willing to experience something does for us. At the moment we become willing to experience it, it no longer feels painful. We are then, in a sense, rid of it.

How can I learn to love' my wants and needs,
especially those that seem to conflict
with others' wants and needs?

I know the problem well. It seems that much of my life has been lived with my own wants and needs kept secret. I see that I do this because I am afraid of the legitimacy of my wants and needs. I am afraid that there is something fundamentally wrong with them. So I keep them to myself and maintain a slight resentment inside.

When I really give myself permission to open up to what I really want, I notice that it does not conflict with what other people want. Usually they feel fine about what I want, or, if they do mind, that opens up a fruitful area of mutual discovery.

We get confused, I think, by believing that if we give ourselves permission to want something, it automatically means we have to *act* on that want. It is valuable to learn the difference between having wants and acting on them. It is essential to passionate living to open up to what we want, to allow ourselves to experience all our wants. But we do not need to act on all our wants, nor could we. The main thing we must do is maintain our integrity with ourselves; this means having no secrets from ourselves. Then, coming from an internal sense of congruence, we can make choices based on what will bring the most positive consequences to all concerned.

It seems like there should be something more we could do other than just loving ourselves.

I know. It seems that loving yourself isn't *doing* very much. There ought to be something more active to do with feelings and other things we need to deal with. Loving yourself, though, seems to be the one thing that we usually forget to do. And naturally it is the one thing that, if we do not do it, will bring us and our growth to a screeching halt. When you are feeling that impatience, that need to *do* something, try loving yourself for feeling that way, then do the most loving thing you can manage.

How does learning to love yourself help you change?

You begin to change the moment you love yourself for being the way you are.

BIOGRAPHICAL NOTE:
Books That Inspired Me

One of the central human myths is that of the person who falls out of harmony with himself or herself, encounters many obstacles as a result, then ultimately learns the lesson at hand. If the person wakes up before it is too late, unity is attained, the lesson learned, and we call it a happy ending. If the person misses the opportunity and wakes up too late, greater disharmony ensues, and we call it tragedy. Viewed in this light, nearly every novel, play, and poem ever written has something to do with learning to love yourself. When I think of works that moved me into greater harmony with myself, books come to mind like Richard Adams' *Watership Down, One Hundred Years of Solitude* by Garcia Marquez, *Another Roadside Attraction* by Tom Robbins, Casteneda's Don Juan series, Gurdjieff's *Meetings with Remarkable Men, Stranger in a Strange Land* by Robert Heinlein, and Frank Herbert's *Dune*. Each of these books creates a view of reality that is either so close to the way things are or so different from the way we usually think of things that we become free for a time of seeing the world in our usual way. Fewer books are directly about the process of coming to love yourself. Rarer still are those books that contain actual instructions for doing so. One book which does, and to which I am eternally grateful, is *The* Lazy Man's *Guide to* Enlightenment, by Thaddeus Golas. This little book has proven valuable to me in so many ways and on so many occasions that I can only say: If you have not read it, please do so. If it has been a while since you have read it, I recommend you read it again. Now, after at least a hundred trips through its eighty jewelstrewn pages, I still think it is one of the great contributions of all time. Wherever you are, Thaddeus, I love you.

Other books that I strongly endorse are *Freedom from the* Known, by Krishnamurti; *The Art of* Loving, by Erich Fromm; *The* Perennial *Philosophy,* by Aldous Huxley; and *The Natural Depth* in Man, by Wilson Van Dusen. Each of these books pointed me along a path deeper into myself; each of them says the same thing in a unique and cherishable way: at the center of us is a clear space that is consonant with the source of all.

Made in the USA
San Bernardino, CA
12 January 2016